Original-Prüfungsaufgaben
mit Lösungen

HAUPTSCHULABSCHLUSS

Englisch 10. Klasse

Nordrhein-Westfalen

2010–2017

MP3-CD

© 2017 Stark Verlag GmbH
8. ergänzte Auflage
www.stark-verlag.de

Das Werk und alle seine Bestandteile sind urheberrechtlich geschützt. Jede vollständige oder teilweise Vervielfältigung, Verbreitung und Veröffentlichung bedarf der ausdrücklichen Genehmigung des Verlages. Dies gilt insbesondere für Vervielfältigungen, Mikroverfilmungen sowie die Speicherung und Verarbeitung in elektronischen Systemen.

Inhalt

Vorwort

Hinweise zur zentralen Prüfung am Ende der Klasse 10

Termine I
Bearbeitungszeit I
Ablauf der schriftlichen Prüfung I
Noten II
Mündliche Prüfung III

Englische Kurzgrammatik

1 Adverbien – *adverbs* .... G 1
2 Bedingungssätze – *conditional sentences* .... G 2
3 Fürwörter – *pronouns* .... G 4
4 Grundform – *infinitive* .... G 5
5 Indirekte Rede – *reported speech* .... G 6
6 Modale Hilfsverben – *modal auxiliaries* .... G 8
7 Konjunktionen – *conjunctions* .... G 9
8 Partizipien – *participles* .... G 10
9 Passiv .... G 12
10 Relativsätze – *relative clauses* .... G 13
11 Steigerung und Vergleich – *comparisons* .... G 13
12 Wortstellung – *word order* .... G 15
13 Zeiten – *tenses* .... G 16
14 Liste wichtiger unregelmäßiger Verben –
   list of irregular verbs .... G 23

Original-Aufgaben der Zentralen Prüfung

Zentrale Prüfung 2010

Hörverstehen 2010-1
Wortschatz – Leseverstehen – Schreiben 2010-5
Lösungsvorschläge 2010-9

Zentrale Prüfung 2011
Hörverstehen 2011-1
Wortschatz – Leseverstehen – Schreiben 2011-4
Lösungsvorschläge 2011-8

Zentrale Prüfung 2012
Hörverstehen – Leseverstehen 2012-1
Wortschatz – Schreiben 2012-5
Lösungsvorschläge 2012-7

Zentrale Prüfung 2013
Hörverstehen – Leseverstehen 2013-1
Wortschatz – Schreiben 2013-5
Lösungsvorschläge 2013-7

Zentrale Prüfung 2014
Hörverstehen – Leseverstehen 2014-1
Wortschatz – Schreiben 2014-5
Lösungsvorschläge 2014-7

Zentrale Prüfung 2015
Hörverstehen – Leseverstehen 2015-1
Wortschatz – Schreiben 2015-5
Lösungsvorschläge 2015-8

Zentrale Prüfung 2016
Hörverstehen – Leseverstehen 2016-1
Wortschatz – Schreiben 2016-5
Lösungsvorschläge 2016-8

Zentrale Prüfung 2017
Hörverstehen – Leseverstehen 2017-1
Wortschatz – Schreiben 2017-5
Lösungsvorschläge 2017-7

MP3-CD

Zentrale Prüfung 2010
Selektives Verstehen: *Phone messages* .... Track 1
Detailliertes Verstehen: *How was your holiday?* .... Track 2
Globales Verstehen: *It drives me crazy* .... Track 3

Zentrale Prüfung 2011
Selektives Verstehen: *Big Ben* .... Track 4
Detailliertes Verstehen: *Living in a skyscraper* .... Track 5
Globales Verstehen: *BBC World News* .... Track 6

Zentrale Prüfung 2012
Hörverstehen Teil 1: *Should teenagers stay in school until
they are 18?* .... Track 7
Hörverstehen Teil 2: *The Green Circle* .... Track 8

Zentrale Prüfung 2013
Hörverstehen Teil 1: *I am sailing* .... Track 9
Hörverstehen Teil 2: *Cool Job – Firefighter* .... Track 10

Zentrale Prüfung 2014
Hörverstehen Teil 1: *The Tube* .... Track 11
Hörverstehen Teil 2: *McDonald's* .... Track 12

Zentrale Prüfung 2015
Hörverstehen Teil 1: *The Brit School* .... Track 13
Hörverstehen Teil 2: *Inuvik Sunrise Festival* .... Track 14

Zentrale Prüfung 2016
Hörverstehen Teil 1: *The Thames Tunnel* .... Track 15
Hörverstehen Teil 2: *How to join Canada's RCMP* .... Track 16

Zentrale Prüfung 2017
Hörverstehen Teil 1: *Hamba Kahle Nelson Mandela* .... Track 17
Hörverstehen Teil 2: *Welcome to Europe?* .... Track 18

*Die Hintergrundgeräusche auf der CD stammen aus folgenden Quellen:
pacdv, Partners in Rhyme, freesound und freesoundeffects*

Sollten nach Erscheinen dieses Bandes noch wichtige Änderungen in der zentralen Prüfung 2018 vom Ministerium für Schule und Weiterbildung bekannt gegeben werden, findest du aktuelle Informationen dazu im Internet unter:
www.stark-verlag.de/pruefung-aktuell

Autor:

Martin Paeslack; Redaktion: Kurzgrammatik

Vorwort

Liebe Schülerin, lieber Schüler,

Prüfungen sind oft mit Unsicherheit verbunden. Dies lässt sich jedoch mit einer langfristigen Vorbereitung vermeiden. In diesem Buch findest du die **Original-Prüfungsaufgaben 2010 bis 2017**. So bietet es dir eine ideale Möglichkeit, dich selbstständig und gezielt auf die **Prüfung 2018** vorzubereiten.

Mithilfe der Original-Prüfungsaufgaben kannst du testen, ob du für den „Ernstfall" gut gerüstet bist. Versuche, eine komplette Aufgabe in 90 Minuten zu bearbeiten – diese Zeit steht dir auch in der Prüfung zur Verfügung. Kontrolliere erst danach deine Lösungen. Hast du viele Fehler gemacht bzw. hat dir die vorgegebene Zeit nicht ausgereicht, arbeite die Aufgaben noch einmal durch. Wenn du nur sehr wenige oder gar keine Fehler gemacht hast, kannst du ganz entspannt in die Prüfung gehen.

Die beiliegende **MP3-CD** enthält die Hörverstehenstexte der Original-Prüfungen. Sie hilft dir dabei, dein Hörverständnis gezielt zu verbessern. Du kannst dich so nicht nur auf die Prüfung, sondern auch auf **Klassenarbeiten und Tests** vorbereiten.

In der **Kurzgrammatik** werden alle wichtigen grammatischen Themen knapp erläutert und an Beispielsätzen veranschaulicht. Hier kannst du nachschlagen, wenn du in der Grammatik einmal unsicher sein solltest.

Der Band „**Training Hauptschulabschluss 2018**" (Best.-Nr. 53550ML) bietet dir weiterführende Übungsmöglichkeiten. Er enthält neben der Original-Prüfung des Jahres 2017 zahlreiche Übungsaufgaben zu allen prüfungsrelevanten Kompetenzbereichen. Darüber hinaus werden dir Strategien zur erfolgreichen Bearbeitung der Aufgaben vermittelt. So kannst du deine sprachlichen Fertigkeiten gezielt trainieren und dich langfristig auf die Prüfung vorbereiten. Das enthaltene ActiveBook, unser interaktives Prüfungstraining, bietet dir darüber hinaus die Möglichkeit, effektiv am Computer oder Tablet zu üben. Wenn du nicht gerne am Computer arbeitest, ist der Band auch ohne ActiveBook erhältlich (Best.-Nr. 53550).

Viel Spaß beim Üben und viel Erfolg in der Prüfung!

Martin Paeslack

Hinweise zur zentralen Prüfung am Ende der Klasse 10

Im Schuljahr 2017/18 finden die zentralen Prüfungen zum Erwerb des Hauptschulabschlusses nach Klasse 10 an folgenden Terminen statt:

Termine
Die Prüfungen finden an folgenden Terminen statt:
Deutsch   8. Mai 2018
Fremdsprache   15. Mai 2018
Mathematik   17. Mai 2018

Bearbeitungszeit
Die Bearbeitungszeiten für die schriftlichen Prüfungen wurden vom Schulministerium folgendermaßen festgelegt:
Deutsch   125 Minuten
Fremdsprache   90 Minuten
Mathematik   90 Minuten

Ablauf der schriftlichen Prüfung
Die schriftliche Prüfung im Fach Englisch besteht aus zwei Teilen.
- Im **ersten Teil** werden die im Laufe der Klassen 5 bis 10 entwickelten **Basiskompetenzen** überprüft. Sie sind – unabhängig von der Schulform – identisch für alle Schülerinnen und Schüler, die auf demselben Abschlussniveau geprüft werden. In der Prüfung 2018 werden das Hör- und Leseverstehen geprüft.
- Im **zweiten Teil** der schriftlichen Prüfung werden Aufgaben gestellt, die **Kompetenzen aus den Jahrgangsstufen 9 und 10** voraussetzen und sich auf die inhaltlichen Schwerpunkte beziehen. Hier musst du u. a. selbst einen Text verfassen. Auch werden dein Wortschatz und/oder deine Grammatikkenntnisse im selben inhaltlichen Kontext geprüft.

Wenn der erste Prüfungsteil nach ca. 40 Minuten abgeschlossen ist, musst du diesen Aufgabenteil abgeben. Du kannst danach also nichts mehr korrigieren. Dann werden die weiteren Aufgaben bearbeitet. Während der gesamten Prüfung wird ein Protokoll geführt, in dem alle Zeiten festgehalten werden (Beginn und Ende der Prüfung; Zeiten, in denen jemand zur Toilette gegangen ist, etc.). Sämtliche besondere Vorkommnisse, wie z. B. ein Täuschungsversuch, werden dort mit der Uhrzeit notiert.

Beachte, dass im Fach Englisch **keine Wörterbücher zugelassen** sind. Die Arbeitsaufgaben und das Papier, auf dem du schreiben kannst, werden dir von der Schule gestellt. Smartphones u. Ä. sind während der Prüfung auch im ausgeschalteten Zustand nicht gestattet und können als Täuschungsversuch gewertet werden. Wichtig ist, dass du Fragen zu Ablauf und Inhalt der Prüfung mit deinem Lehrer/deiner Lehrerin besprichst und genau zuhörst. Schreibe dir dabei die wichtigen Informationen auf, damit du sie nicht vergisst. Du wirst in der Prüfung Aufgaben erhalten, die mit **Großbritannien und Südafrika** zu tun haben. Es ist also hilfreich, sich über diese beiden Länder genauer zu informieren. Du findest dazu Informationen in den Schulbüchern. Darüber hinaus kannst du auch im Internet recherchieren, ein passendes Buch lesen oder eine interessante Sendung im Fernsehen anschauen.

Noten

Deine Abschlussnote setzt sich aus der Prüfungsnote als Ergebnis deiner schriftlichen Prüfung und der Vornote zusammen. Diese Note beruht auf **allen** Leistungen seit Beginn des Schuljahres. Auch Hausaufgaben, mündliche Leistungen, Mitarbeit, Heftführung, Referate, Gruppenarbeitsergebnisse zählen zu diesen Leistungen.
- Stimmen Vornote und Prüfungsnote überein, ist die Vornote auch die Abschlussnote.
- Bei einer Abweichung von einer Note entscheidet dein Fachlehrer zwischen beiden Noten. Falls Vornote und Prüfungsnote um zwei Noten voneinander abweichen, kannst du dich einer freiwilligen mündlichen Prüfung im Fach Englisch unterziehen. Falls du das nicht möchtest, wird der Mittelwert aus Vornote und Prüfungsnote gebildet. Du solltest aber unbedingt mit deinem Fachlehrer besprechen, ob es in deiner Situation Sinn macht, sich für die mündliche Prüfung anzumelden.
- Weicht deine Prüfungsnote um mehr als zwei Notenstufen von der Vornote ab, ist die mündliche Prüfung für dich verpflichtend.

Die Bewertung deiner schriftlichen Prüfung erfolgt durch die Vergabe von Punkten. Den Arbeiten wird eine Tabelle zur Umrechnung der Punktwerte in Noten beigefügt. Dabei werden der erste und zweite Teil entsprechend der vorgesehenen Bearbeitungsdauer gewichtet.

Grundsätzlich geht man davon aus, dass
- die Note „ausreichend" das Erreichen von 45 % der Höchstpunktzahl voraussetzt,

- oberhalb der Note „ausreichend" die Zuordnung der Punktzahlen zu den Notenstufen linear verteilt ist,
- die Grenze zwischen den Noten „mangelhaft" und „ungenügend" bei etwa 18 % der Höchstpunktzahl liegt.

Mündliche Prüfung

Die mündliche Prüfung ist bei einer Abweichung von zwei Noten freiwillig. Nur bei zu starker Abweichung bist du verpflichtet, die mündliche Prüfung abzulegen. Sie findet im Zeitraum vom 25. Juni 2018 bis zum 3. Juli 2018 statt.
Sie wird nicht zentral vom Schulministerium gestellt, d. h., dein Englischlehrer oder deine Englischlehrerin formuliert die mündlichen Prüfungsaufgaben selbst. Geprüft wird der Stoff der Klasse 10, allerdings so, dass sich keine Überschneidungen zur schriftlichen Prüfung ergeben. Die Fachlehrerin/der Fachlehrer benennt drei Unterrichtsvorhaben aus der Jahrgangsstufe 10 als inhaltliche Grundlage. Die Aufgabenstellungen werden dir schriftlich vorgelegt. In einer etwa 10-minütigen Vorbereitungszeit kannst du dich mit der Aufgabenstellung auseinandersetzen. Das Prüfungsgespräch dauert 15 Minuten und könnte sich folgendermaßen zusammensetzen:

1. Einstimmungsphase (ca. 3 Minuten): Es werden allgemeine Fragen gestellt wie "How are you?" oder "What did you have for breakfast?".
2. Zusammenhängendes Sprechen (ca. 6 Minuten): Du sollst hier zu einem vertrauten Thema sprechen. Zur Vorbereitung bekommst du z. B. eine Mindmap oder einen kurzen Text vorgelegt.
3. Gespräch: Hier führst du ein Gespräch mit deinem Lehrer/deiner Lehrerin, z. B. über ein Bild, das dir vorgelegt wird.

Dein Englischlehrer oder deine Englischlehrerin kann Zwischenfragen stellen, wenn er/sie etwas genauer von dir wissen möchte oder wenn dir zu einem Thema nicht so viel einfällt. Die Zeugnisnote setzt sich im Fall einer mündlichen Prüfung aus drei Noten zusammen:
- Vornote
- Note für die schriftliche Prüfungsleistung
- Note für die mündliche Prüfungsleistung

Diese Noten werden gewichtet im Verhältnis
5 (Vornote) : 3 (schriftliche Prüfung) : 2 (mündliche Prüfung)

Eine weitere Nachprüfung ist in den Prüfungsfächern **nicht möglich**. Das bedeutet vor allem, dass du dich in den Fächern, in denen du eine Abschlussprüfung gemacht hast, nicht zu einer weiteren mündlichen Prüfung anmelden kannst, um zum Beispiel noch die Qualifikation für die Sekundarstufe II zu erreichen. Dies geht nur in den anderen Fächern.

Kurzgrammatik

1 Adverbien – *adverbs*

Bildung
Adjektiv + *-ly*   glad   → glad<u>ly</u>

Ausnahmen:
- *-y* am Wortende wird zu *-i*   easy   → eas<u>i</u>ly
                                               funny   → funn<u>i</u>ly
- auf einen Konsonanten folgendes *-le* wird zu *-ly*   simp<u>le</u> → simp<u>ly</u>
                                               terrib<u>le</u> → terrib<u>ly</u>
- am Wortende wird *-ic* zu *-ically*   fantast<u>ic</u> → fantast<u>ically</u>

Beachte:
- In einigen Fällen haben Adjektiv und Adverb dieselbe Form.   daily, early, fast, hard, long, low, weekly, yearly
- Unregelmäßig gebildet wird: good   → well
- Endet das Adjektiv auf *-ly*, so kannst du kein Adverb bilden und verwendest deshalb: *in a* + Adjektiv + *manner*   friendly → <u>in a friendly</u> manner

Verwendung
Adverbien bestimmen z. B.
- Verben   She <u>easily found</u> her way.
                                               Sie hat sich leicht zurechtgefunden.
- Adjektive oder   This band is <u>extremely famous</u>.
                                               Diese Band ist sehr berühmt.
- andere Adverbien   He walks <u>extremely quickly</u>.
                                               Er geht äußerst schnell.

näher.

Beachte: Nach bestimmten Verben (z. B. *to be, to become, to feel, to smell, to look*) steht ein Adjektiv.

Peter is funny.
Peter ist lustig.
I feel cold.
Mir ist kalt.

2 Bedingungssätze – *conditional sentences*

Ein Bedingungssatz besteht aus zwei Teilen: Nebensatz (*if*-Satz) + Hauptsatz. Im ***if*-Satz** steht die **Bedingung**, unter der die im **Hauptsatz** genannte **Folge** eintritt. Man unterscheidet drei Arten von Bedingungssätzen:

Bedingungssatz Typ I

Bildung
- *if*-Satz (Bedingung): Gegenwart *(simple present)*
- Hauptsatz (Folge): Zukunft mit *will (will-future)*

If you read this book,
Wenn du dieses Buch liest,
you will learn a lot about music.
erfährst du eine Menge über Musik.

Der *if*-Satz kann auch nach dem Hauptsatz stehen:
- Hauptsatz: *will-future*

You will learn a lot about music
Du erfährst eine Menge über Musik,

- *if*-Satz: *simple present*

if you read this book.
wenn du dieses Buch liest.

Im Hauptsatz kann statt dem *will-future* auch
- *can* + Grundform des Verbs,

If you go to London, you can see Bob.
Wenn du nach London fährst, kannst du Bob treffen.

- *must* + Grundform des Verbs,

If you go to London, you must visit me.
Wenn du nach London fährst, musst du mich besuchen.

- die Befehlsform (Imperativ)

stehen.

If it rains, take an umbrella.
Wenn es regnet, nimm einen Schirm mit.

Verwendung
Bedingungssätze vom Typ I verwendet man, wenn die **Bedingung erfüllbar** ist. Man gibt an, was unter bestimmten Bedingungen **geschieht, geschehen kann** oder was **geschehen sollte**.

Bedingungssatz Typ II

Bildung
- *if*-Satz (Bedingung):
  1. Vergangenheit *(simple past)*
- Hauptsatz (Folge): Konditional I
  (conditional I = would + Grundform des Verbs*)*

If I <u>went</u> to London,
Wenn ich nach London fahren würde,
I <u>would visit</u> the Tower of London.
würde ich mir den Tower of London ansehen.

Verwendung
Bedingungssätze vom Typ II verwendet man, wenn die **Bedingung theoretisch erfüllt** werden kann oder **nicht erfüllbar** ist.

Bedingungssatz Typ III

Bildung
- *if*-Satz (Bedingung): Vorvergangenheit *(past perfect)*
- Hauptsatz (Folge): Konditional II
  (conditional II = would + have + past participle)

If I <u>had gone</u> to London,
Wenn ich nach London gefahren wäre,
I <u>would have visited</u> the Tower of London.
hätte ich mir den Tower of London angesehen.

Verwendung
Bedingungssätze vom Typ III verwendet man, wenn sich die **Bedingung auf die Vergangenheit bezieht** und deshalb **nicht mehr erfüllbar** ist.

3 Fürwörter – *pronouns*

Besitzanzeigende Fürwörter – *possessive pronouns*

Besitzanzeigende Fürwörter *(possessive pronouns)* verwendet man, um zu sagen, **wem etwas gehört**. Steht ein besitzanzeigendes Fürwort allein, verwendest du eine andere Form:

mit Substantiv	ohne Substantiv		
my	*mine*	This is <u>my</u> bike. –	This is <u>mine</u>.
your	*yours*	This is <u>your</u> bike. –	This is <u>yours</u>.
his / her / its	*his / hers / ...*	This is <u>her</u> bike. –	This is <u>hers</u>.
our	*ours*	This is <u>our</u> bike. –	This is <u>ours</u>.
your	*yours*	This is <u>your</u> bike. –	This is <u>yours</u>.
their	*theirs*	This is <u>their</u> bike. –	This is <u>theirs</u>.

Rückbezügliche Fürwörter – *reflexive pronouns*

Die rückbezüglichen Fürwörter *(reflexive pronouns)* **beziehen sich auf das Subjekt** des Satzes **zurück**. Es handelt sich also um dieselbe Person.

myself	<u>I</u> will buy <u>myself</u> a new car.
	<u>Ich</u> werde <u>mir</u> ein neues Auto kaufen.
yourself	<u>You</u> will buy <u>yourself</u> a new car.
himself / herself / itself	<u>He</u> will buy <u>himself</u> a new car.
ourselves	<u>We</u> will buy <u>ourselves</u> a new car.
yourselves	<u>You</u> will buy <u>yourselves</u> a new car.
themselves	<u>They</u> will buy <u>themselves</u> a new car.

each other/one another

> *each other/one another* ist unveränderlich. Es bezieht sich auf **zwei oder mehr Personen** und wird mit „sich (gegenseitig), einander" übersetzt.
>
> **Beachte:**
> Einige Verben stehen ohne *each other*, obwohl auf Deutsch mit „sich" übersetzt wird.

They looked at <u>each other</u> and laughed.
Sie schauten sich (gegenseitig) an und lachten.
oder:
Sie schauten einander an und lachten.

to meet	*sich treffen*
to kiss	*sich küssen*
to fall in love	*sich verlieben*

4 Grundform – *infinitive*

> Die Grundform mit *to* steht nach
> - bestimmten Verben, z. B.:
>
> | | |
> |---|---|
> | *to agree* | zustimmen |
> | *to choose* | wählen |
> | *to decide* | entscheiden |
> | *to expect* | erwarten |
> | *to hope* | hoffen |
> | *to offer* | anbieten |
> | *to plan* | planen |
> | *to promise* | versprechen |
> | *to seem* | scheinen |
> | *to want* | wollen |
>
> - bestimmten Substantiven, z. B.:
>
> | | |
> |---|---|
> | *idea* | Idee |
> | *plan* | Plan |
> | *wish* | Wunsch |
>
> - bestimmten Adjektiven, z. B.:
>
> | | |
> |---|---|
> | *certain* | sicher |
> | *difficult* | schwer, schwierig |
> | *easy* | leicht |
> | *hard* | schwer, schwierig |

He <u>decided</u> <u>to wait</u>.
Er beschloss zu warten.

It was her <u>wish</u> <u>to marry</u> in November.
Es war ihr Wunsch, im November zu heiraten.

It was <u>difficult</u> <u>to follow</u> her.
Es war schwer, ihr zu folgen.

- den Fragewörtern *what, where, which, who, when, why, how* in einer indirekten Frage.

We knew <u>where</u> <u>to find</u> her.
Wir wussten, wo wir sie finden würden.

5 Indirekte Rede – *reported speech*

Die indirekte Rede verwendet man, um **wiederzugeben, was ein anderer gesagt** oder **gefragt hat**.

Bildung
Um die indirekte Rede zu bilden, benötigt man ein **Einleitungsverb**. Häufig verwendete Einleitungsverben sind:

to say, to tell, to add, to agree, to think, to ask, to want to know, to answer

In der indirekten Rede verändern sich die Fürwörter (Pronomen), in bestimmten Fällen auch die **Zeiten** und die **Orts-** und **Zeitangaben**.

- **Veränderung der Fürwörter:**
  persönliche Fürwörter:
  besitzanzeigende Fürwörter:
  hinweisende Fürwörter:

direkte Rede	indirekte Rede
I, you, we, you	he, she, they
my, your, our, your	his, her, their
this, these	that, those

- **Zeiten**
  Keine Veränderung, wenn das **Einleitungsverb** in der **Gegenwart** *(simple present)* oder im *present perfect* steht:

direkte Rede	indirekte Rede
Bob <u>says</u>, "I <u>love</u> dancing."	Bob <u>says</u> (that) he <u>loves</u> dancing.
Bob sagt: „Ich tanze sehr gerne."	*Bob sagt, er tanze sehr gerne.*

Die Zeit der direkten Rede wird in der indirekten Rede **um eine Zeitstufe zurückversetzt**, wenn das **Einleitungsverb** im *simple past* steht:

direkte Rede	indirekte Rede
Bob <u>said</u>, "I <u>love</u> dancing."	Bob <u>said</u> (that) he <u>loved</u> dancing.
Bob sagte: „Ich tanze sehr gerne."	*Bob sagte, er tanze sehr gerne.*

direkte Rede	indirekte Rede
simple present	*simple past*
simple past	*past perfect*
present perfect	*past perfect*
will-future	*conditional I*

Joe: "I like it." — Joe said he liked it.
Joe: "I liked it." — Joe said he had liked it.
Joe: "I've liked it." — Joe said he had liked it.
Joe: "I will like it." — Joe said he would like it.

- Veränderung der Orts- und Zeitangaben:

now	→	then
today	→	that day
yesterday	→	the day before
the day before yesterday	→	two days before
tomorrow	→	the following day
next week	→	the following week
here	→	there

Bildung der indirekten Frage
Häufige Einleitungsverben für die indirekte Frage sind *to ask* oder *to want to know*.

- Enthält die direkte Frage ein **Fragewort, bleibt** dieses in der indirekten Frage **erhalten**. Die **Umschreibung** mit *do/does/did* **entfällt** in der indirekten Frage.

Tom: "When did they arrive?" — Tom asked when they had arrived.
Tom: „Wann sind sie angekommen?" — Tom fragte, wann sie angekommen seien.

- Enthält die direkte Frage **kein Fragewort**, wird die indirekte Frage mit *whether* oder *if* eingeleitet:

Tom: "Are they staying at the hotel?" — Tom asked if/whether they were staying at the hotel.
Tom: „Übernachten sie im Hotel?" — Tom fragte, ob sie im Hotel übernachten.

Befehle/Aufforderungen in der indirekten Rede
Häufige Einleitungsverben sind *to tell*, *to order* (Befehl), *to ask* (Aufforderung).

In der indirekten Rede steht hier **Einleitungsverb + Objekt + *(not) to* + Grundform des Verbs** der direkten Rede.	Tom: "Leave the room." Tom: „Verlass den Raum."	Tom told me to leave the room. Tom forderte mich auf, den Raum zu verlassen.

6 Modale Hilfsverben – *modal auxiliaries*

Zu den **modalen Hilfsverben** *(modal auxiliaries)* zählen z. B. *can, may* und *must*.

Bildung
- Die modalen Hilfsverben haben für alle Personen **nur eine Form**.

  I, you, he/she/it, we, you, they } must

- Auf das modale Hilfsverb folgt die **Grundform** des Verbs **ohne *to***.

  You must listen to my new CD.
  Du musst dir meine neue CD anhören.

- **Frage und Verneinung** werden **nicht** mit *do/does/did* umschrieben.

  Can you help me, please?
  Kannst du mir bitte helfen?

Die modalen Hilfsverben können nicht alle Zeiten bilden. Deshalb benötigt man bestimmte **Ersatzformen**. Diese Ersatzformen können auch im Präsens verwendet werden.

- ***can*** (können)
  Ersatzformen:
  (to) be able to (Fähigkeit),
  (to) be allowed to (Erlaubnis)

  I can sing. / I was able to sing.
  Ich kann singen. / Ich konnte singen.

  You can't go to the party. /
  I wasn't allowed to go to the party.
  Du darfst nicht auf die Party gehen. /
  Ich durfte nicht auf die Party gehen.

Im *simple past* und *conditional I* kannst du auch *could* verwenden.

- **may** (dürfen)
  Ersatzform: ***(to) be allowed to***

- **must** (müssen)
  Ersatzform: ***(to) have to***

  Beachte:
  must not/mustn't = „nicht dürfen"

  „nicht müssen, nicht brauchen" = **not have to, needn't**

I could sing.
Ich konnte singen.

You may go home early today. / You were allowed to go home early yesterday.
Du darfst heute früh nach Hause gehen. / Du durftest gestern früh nach Hause gehen.

He must be home by ten o'clock. / He had to be home by ten o'clock.
Er muss bis zehn Uhr zu Hause sein. / Er musste bis zehn Uhr zu Hause sein.

You must not eat all the cake.
Du darfst nicht den ganzen Kuchen essen.

You don't have to / needn't eat all the cake.
Du musst nicht den ganzen Kuchen essen./ Du brauchst nicht ... zu essen.

7 Konjunktionen – *conjunctions*

Konjunktionen *(conjunctions)* sind Bindewörter, die **zwei Hauptsätze oder Haupt- und Nebensatz miteinander verbinden**. Mit Konjunktionen lässt sich ein Text strukturieren, indem man z. B. Ursachen, Folgen oder zeitliche Abfolgen angibt. Hier findest du einige Beispiele für Konjunktionen:

after	– nachdem	What will you do after she's gone? *Was wirst du tun, nachdem sie gegangen ist?*
although	– obwohl	I like my bike although it's old. *Ich mag mein Fahrrad, obwohl es alt ist.*
because	– weil	I need a new bike because my old bike was stolen. *Ich brauche ein neues Rad, weil mein altes Rad gestohlen wurde.*

before	– bevor	Before he goes to work, he buys a newspaper. *Bevor er zur Arbeit geht, kauft er eine Zeitung.*
but	– aber	She likes football but she doesn't like skiing. *Sie mag Fußball, aber sie fährt nicht gerne Ski.*
that	– dass	It is nice that you are here. *Es ist schön, dass du hier bist.*
then	– dann	He bought an ice cream, and then shared it with Sally. *Er kaufte ein Eis, (und) dann teilte er es mit Sally.*
when	– wenn, als (zeitlich)	Tell me when you've finished. *Sag mir, wenn du fertig bist.* It rained when I was in Paris. *Es regnete, als ich in Paris war.*
while	– während, solange	While we were in London, we had very good weather. *Während wir in London waren, hatten wir sehr gutes Wetter.*

8 Partizipien – *participles*

Partizip Präsens – *present participle*

Bildung
Grundform des Verbs + *-ing*   read → read*ing*

Beachte:
- Stummes *-e* entfällt.   writ*e* → writ*ing*
- Verdoppelung des Schlusskonsonanten nach kurzem Vokal   sto*p* → sto*pp*ing
- *-ie* wird zu *-y*.   l*ie* → l*y*ing

Verwendung
Das Partizip Präsens *(present participle)* verwendet man u. a.

- zur Bildung der Verlaufsform der Gegenwart *(present progressive)*,

  Peter <u>is reading</u>.
  Peter liest (gerade).

- zur Bildung der Verlaufsform der Vergangenheit *(past progressive)*.

  She <u>was reading</u> when I came back.
  Sie las (gerade), als ich zurückkam.

- wie ein Adjektiv, wenn es vor einem Substantiv steht.

  The village hasn't got <u>running</u> water.
  Das Dorf hat kein fließendes Wasser.

Partizip Perfekt – past *participle*

Bildung
Grundform des Verbs + *-ed*

talk → talk<u>ed</u>

Beachte:

- Stummes *-e* entfällt.

  liv<u>e</u> → liv<u>ed</u>

- Nach kurzem betontem Vokal wird der Schlusskonsonant verdoppelt.

  sto<u>p</u> → sto<u>pp</u>ed

- *-y* wird zu *-ie*.

  cr<u>y</u> → cr<u>ie</u>d

- Unregelmäßige Verben: siehe Liste S. G 23 f. Hier sind bereits die *past-participle*-Formen der wichtigsten unregelmäßigen Verben angegeben:

  be → been
  have → had
  give → given
  go → gone

Verwendung
Das Partizip Perfekt *(past participle)* verwendet man u. a.

- zur Bildung des *present perfect*,

  He <u>hasn't talked</u> to his father yet.
  Er hat noch nicht mit seinem Vater gesprochen.

- zur Bildung des *past perfect*,

- zur Bildung des Passivs.

- wie ein Adjektiv, wenn es vor einem Substantiv steht.

Before they went to France, they <u>had</u> <u>bought</u> new bikes.
Bevor sie nach Frankreich fuhren, hatten sie neue Fahrräder gekauft.

The fish was <u>eaten</u> by the cat.
Der Fisch wurde von der Katze gefressen.

Peter has got a well-<u>paid</u> job.
Peter hat eine gut bezahlte Stelle.

9 Passiv

Bildung
Form von *(to) be* + Partizip Perfekt

- im *simple present*

- im *simple past*

The bridge <u>was finished</u> in 1894.
Die Brücke wurde 1894 fertiggestellt.

Aktiv: Joe <u>buys</u> the milk.
Passiv: The milk <u>is</u> <u>bought</u> by Joe.

Aktiv: Joe <u>bought</u> the milk.
Passiv: The milk <u>was</u> <u>bought</u> by Joe.

Aktiv → Passiv

Bei der Umwandlung vom Aktiv ins Passiv ...

- ... wird das Subjekt des Aktivsatzes zum Objekt des Passivsatzes. Es wird mit *by* angeschlossen *(by-agent)*.

- ... wird das Objekt des Aktivsatzes zum Subjekt des Passivsatzes.

Aktiv: <u>Joe</u>   buys   <u>the milk.</u>
         Subjekt   *Objekt*

Passiv: <u>The milk</u> is bought <u>by Joe.</u>
          Subjekt   *by-agent*

10 Relativsätze – *relative clauses*

Ein Relativsatz ist ein Nebensatz, der sich auf eine **Person oder Sache des Hauptsatzes** bezieht und diese **näher beschreibt**:
- Hauptsatz:
- Relativsatz:

The boy who looks like Jane is her brother.
Der Junge, der Jane ähnlich sieht, ist ihr Bruder.
The boy ... is her brother
... who looks like Jane ...

Bildung
Haupt- und Nebensatz werden durch ein Relativpronomen *(who, which, that)* verbunden.

- *who* bezieht sich auf **Personen**,

Peter, who lives in London, likes travelling.
Peter, der in London lebt, reist gerne.

- *which* bezieht sich auf **Sachen**,

The film "Dark Moon", which we saw yesterday, was far too long.
Der Film „Dark Moon", den wir gestern sahen, war viel zu lang.

- *that* kann sich auf **Sachen** und in der Umgangssprache auch auf **Personen** beziehen.

The film that we saw last week was much better.
Der Film, den wir letzte Woche sahen, war viel besser.

11 Steigerung und Vergleich – *comparisons*

Steigerung des Adjektivs – *comparison of adjectives*

Bildung
Man unterscheidet:
- Grundform
- 1. Steigerungsform (Komparativ)
- 2. Steigerungsform (Superlativ)

Peter is young.
Jane is younger.
Paul is the youngest.

Steigerung auf -*er*, -*est*
Bei den meisten einsilbigen und zweisilbigen Adjektiven, z. B.:

old, old<u>er</u>, old<u>est</u>
alt, älter, am ältesten

funny, funn<u>ie</u>r, funn<u>ie</u>st
lustig, lustiger, am lustigsten

Beachte:
- stummes -*e* am Wortende entfällt
- nach einem Konsonanten wird -*y* am Wortende zu -*i*-
- nach kurzem Vokal wird ein Konsonant am Wortende verdoppelt

simpl<u>e</u>, simpl<u>er</u>, simpl<u>est</u>

funn<u>y</u>, funn<u>ie</u>r, funn<u>ie</u>st

fi<u>t</u>, fi<u>tt</u>er, fi<u>tt</u>est

Steigerung mit *more ..., most ...*
- zweisilbige Adjektive, die nicht auf -*er*, -*le*, -*ow* oder -*y* enden
- Adjektive mit drei und mehr Silben

useful, <u>more</u> useful, <u>most</u> useful
nützlich, nützlicher, am nützlichsten

difficult, <u>more</u> difficult, <u>most</u> difficult
schwierig, schwieriger, am schwierigsten

Unregelmäßige Steigerung
Die unregelmäßig gesteigerten Adjektive solltest du lernen. Einige wichtige Adjektive sind hier angegeben.

good, better, best
gut, besser, am besten

bad, worse, worst
schlecht, schlechter, am schlechtesten

many, more, most
viele, mehr, am meisten

much, more, most
viel, mehr, am meisten

little, less, least
wenig, weniger, am wenigsten

Vergleiche von Personen und Dingen

Bildung

- Wenn du sagen möchtest, dass Personen oder Dinge **gleich** sind:
  as + Adjektiv (Grundform) + as

  Anne is <u>as</u> tall <u>as</u> John.
  Anne ist genauso groß wie John.

- Wenn du sagen möchtest, dass Personen oder Dinge **ungleich** sind: *not as* + Adjektiv (Grundform) + *as*

  John is <u>not as</u> tall <u>as</u> Steve.
  John ist nicht so groß wie Steve.

- Wenn du sagen möchtest, dass Personen oder Dinge **verschieden** gut/schlecht/ schön ... sind:
  1. Steigerungsform (Komparativ) des Adjektivs + *than*

  Steve is <u>taller</u> than Anne.
  Steve ist größer als Anne.

Steigerung des Adverbs – *comparison of adverbs*

Adverbien können wie Adjektive ebenfalls gesteigert werden.

- Adverbien auf *-ly* werden mit ***more, most*** bzw. mit ***less, least*** gesteigert.

  She talks <u>more</u> <u>quickly</u> than John.
  Sie spricht schneller als John.

- Adverbien, die dieselbe Form wie das Adjektiv haben, werden mit ***-er, -est*** gesteigert.

  fast – fast<u>er</u> – fast<u>est</u>
  early – earli<u>er</u> – earli<u>est</u>

- Folgende Adverbien haben unregelmäßige Steigerungsformen:

  well – better – best
  badly – worse – worst

12 Wortstellung – *word order*

Im englischen Aussagesatz gilt die Wortstellung <u>Su</u>bjekt – <u>Prä</u>dikat – <u>O</u>bjekt *(subject – verb – object):*

- Das <u>Subjekt</u> gibt an, wer oder was etwas tut.
- Das <u>Prädikat</u> gibt an, was getan wird.
- Das <u>Objekt</u> gibt an, worauf/auf wen sich die Tätigkeit bezieht.

<u>The cat</u>
Die Katze
<u>catches</u>
fängt
<u>a mouse</u>.
eine Maus.

Beachte:
- Orts- und Zeitangaben stehen meist am Satzende.

We will buy a new car <u>tomorrow</u>.
Morgen kaufen wir ein neues Auto.
Peter lives <u>in New York</u>.
Peter wohnt in New York.

- Ortsangaben stehen vor Zeitangaben.

He moved <u>to Paris</u> <u>in June</u>.
Er ist im Juni nach Paris gezogen.

13 Zeiten – *tenses*

Gegenwart – *simple present*

Bildung
Grundform des Verbs,
Ausnahme 3. Person Singular:
Grundform des Verbs + *-s*

Beachte:
- Bei Verben, die auf *-s, -sh, -ch, -x* enden, wird *-es* angefügt.

- Bei Verben, die auf Konsonant + *-y* enden, wird *-es* angefügt; *-y* wird zu *-i-*.

stand – he/she/it stand<u>s</u>
kiss – he/she/it kiss<u>es</u>
rush – he/she/it rush<u>es</u>
teach – he/she/it teach<u>es</u>
fix – he/she/it fix<u>es</u>
carry – he/she/it carr<u>ies</u>

Bildung von Fragen im *simple present*
(Fragewort +) *do/does* + Grundform des Verbs

<u>Where</u> <u>does</u> he <u>live</u>? / <u>Does</u> he <u>live</u> in London?
Wo lebt er? / Lebt er in London?

Beachte:
Die Umschreibung mit *do/does* wird nicht verwendet,
- wenn nach dem Subjekt gefragt wird (mit *who, what, which*).

Who likes pizza?
Wer mag Pizza?
What happens next?
Was passiert als Nächstes?

- wenn die Frage mit *is/are* gebildet wird.

Are you happy?
Bist du glücklich?

Bildung der Verneinung im *simple present*
don't/doesn't + Grundform des Verbs

He doesn't like football.
Er mag Fußball nicht.

Verwendung
Das *simple present* beschreibt
- Tätigkeiten, die man **gewohnheitsmäßig** oder häufig (oder gar nicht) ausführt.
  Signalwörter: z. B. *always, often, never, every day, every morning*

Every morning John buys a newspaper.
Jeden Morgen kauft sich John eine Zeitung.

- **allgemeingültige** Aussagen.

London is a big city.
London ist eine große Stadt.

- **Eigenschaften** und **Zustände** von Personen und Dingen, z. B. *to like, to hate, to know*

I like dogs.
Ich mag Hunde.

- ein **zukünftiges Geschehen** mit einem festen Termin (z. B. Fahrpläne, Kalender).

The train leaves at 8.15.
Der Zug fährt um 8.15 Uhr.

The holidays start next week.
Nächste Woche fangen die Ferien an.

Verlaufsform des *simple present* – *present progressive/continuous*

Bildung
am/is/are + Verb in der *-ing*-Form (Partizip Präsens)

read → am/is/are reading

Bildung von Fragen im *present progressive*
(Fragewort +) *am/is/are* + Subjekt + Verb in der *-ing*-Form

<u>Is</u> Peter <u>reading</u>? / <u>What is</u> he <u>reading</u>?
Liest Peter gerade? / Was liest er?

Bildung der Verneinung im *present progressive*
am not/isn't/aren't + Verb in der *-ing*-Form

Peter <u>isn't</u> <u>reading</u>.
Peter liest gerade nicht.

Verwendung
Mit dem *present progressive* drückt man aus,
- dass etwas **gerade passiert** und **noch nicht abgeschlossen** ist. Signalwörter: *at the moment, now*

At the moment, Peter <u>is drinking</u> a cup of tea.
Im Augenblick trinkt Peter eine Tasse Tee. [Er hat damit angefangen und noch nicht aufgehört.]

- dass es um eine **zukünftige Handlung** geht, die bereits **fest geplant** ist.

We <u>are watching</u> the match on Sunday.
Am Sonntag sehen wir uns das Spiel an.

Simple past

Bildung
Regelmäßige Verben:
Grundform des Verbs + *-ed*

walk → walk<u>ed</u>

Beachte:
- Stummes *-e* entfällt.
- Bei Verben, die auf Konsonant + *-y* enden, wird *-y* zu *-i-*.

hop<u>e</u> → hop<u>ed</u>
car<u>ry</u> → carr<u>ied</u>

- Nach kurzem betontem Vokal wird der Schlusskonsonant verdoppelt.

sto<u>p</u> → sto<u>pped</u>

Unregelmäßige Verben: siehe Liste S. G 23 f. Hier sind bereits die *simple past*-Formen der wichtigsten unregelmäßigen Verben angegeben:

be → was
have → had
give → gave
go → went

Bildung von Fragen im *simple past*
(Fragewort +) *did* + Grundform des Verbs

<u>Did</u> he <u>look</u> out of the window?
<u>Why</u> <u>did</u> he <u>look</u> out of the window?
Sah er aus dem Fenster?
Warum sah er aus dem Fenster?

Beachte:
Die Umschreibung mit *did* wird nicht verwendet,
- wenn nach dem Subjekt gefragt wird (mit *who, what, which*),

<u>Who</u> <u>paid</u> the bill?
Wer zahlte die Rechnung?

<u>What</u> <u>happened</u> to your friend?
Was ist mit deinem Freund passiert?

<u>Which</u> boy <u>cooked</u> the meal?
Welcher Junge kochte das Essen?

- wenn die Frage mit *was/were* gebildet wird.

<u>Were</u> you happy?
Warst du glücklich?

Bildung der Verneinung im *simple past*
didn't + Grundform des Verbs

He <u>didn't</u> <u>call</u> me.
Er hat mich nicht angerufen.

Verwendung
Das *simple past* beschreibt Handlungen und Ereignisse, die **in der Vergangenheit geschehen** und **bereits abgeschlossen** sind.

Last week he <u>helped</u> me with my homework.
Letzte Woche half er mir bei meinen Hausaufgaben. [Die Handlung (helfen) fand in der letzten Woche statt, ist also bereits abgeschlossen.]

Signalwörter: z. B. *yesterday, last week, (five years) ago, in 2008*

Verlaufsform des *simple past* – *past progressive/continuous*

Bildung
was/were + Verb in der *-ing*-Form

watch → <u>was/were</u> watch<u>ing</u>

Verwendung
Das *past progressive* verwendet man, wenn **zu einem bestimmten Zeitpunkt** in der Vergangenheit eine **Handlung ablief**, bzw. wenn eine **Handlung** von einer anderen **unterbrochen** wurde.

Yesterday at 11 o'clock I <u>was</u> still <u>sleeping</u>.
Gestern um 11 Uhr habe ich noch geschlafen.
I <u>was reading</u> a book when Peter came into the room.
Ich las (gerade) ein Buch, als Peter ins Zimmer kam.

Present perfect

Bildung
have/has + Partizip Perfekt

write → <u>has/have</u> <u>written</u>

Verwendung
Das *present perfect* verwendet man, wenn
- ein Vorgang **in der Vergangenheit begonnen** hat und **noch andauert**.

He <u>has lived</u> in London since 2008.
Er lebt seit 2008 in London.
[Er lebt jetzt immer noch in London.]

- das Ergebnis einer vergangenen Handlung **Auswirkungen auf die Gegenwart** hat.

I <u>have tidied up</u> my room.
Ich habe mein Zimmer aufgeräumt.
[Jetzt sieht es wieder ordentlich aus.]

Signalwörter: z. B. *already, ever, just, how long, not ... yet, since, for*

Beachte:
- *have/has* können zu *'ve/'s* verkürzt werden.

I<u>'ve</u> eaten your lunch.
Ich habe dein Mittagessen gegessen.
He<u>'s</u> given me his umbrella.
Er hat mir seinen Schirm gegeben.

- Das *present perfect* wird oft mit *since* und *for* verwendet (Deutsch: „seit"):
  since gibt einen **Zeitpunkt** an: Ron has lived in Sydney <u>since 1997</u>.
  Ron lebt seit 1997 in Sydney.

- *for* gibt einen **Zeitraum** an: Sally has lived in Berlin <u>for five years</u>.
  Sally lebt seit fünf Jahren in Berlin.

Verlaufsform des *present perfect* – *present perfect progressive/continuous*

Bildung
have/has + been + Partizip Präsens   write → <u>has/have</u> <u>been</u> <u>writing</u>

Verwendung
Das *present perfect progressive* verwendet man, um die **Dauer einer Handlung** zu **betonen**, die in der Vergangenheit begonnen hat und noch andauert.

She <u>has been sleeping</u> for ten hours.
Sie schläft seit zehn Stunden.

Past perfect

Bildung
had + Partizip Perfekt   write → <u>had</u> <u>written</u>

Verwendung
Das *past perfect* verwendet man, wenn ein Vorgang in der Vergangenheit **vor einem anderen Vorgang in der Vergangenheit abgeschlossen** wurde.

He <u>had bought</u> a ticket
Er hatte ein Ticket gekauft,

before he took the train to Manchester.
bevor er den Zug nach Manchester nahm. [Beim Einsteigen war der Kauf abgeschlossen.]

Verlaufsform des *past perfect* – *past perfect progressive/continuous*

Bildung
had + *been* + Partizip Präsens

write → had been writing

Verwendung
Das *past perfect progressive* verwendet man für **Handlungen**, die in der Vergangenheit **bis zu dem Zeitpunkt andauerten**, zu dem eine neue Handlung einsetzte.

She had been sleeping for ten hours when the doorbell rang.
Sie hatte seit zehn Stunden geschlafen, als es an der Tür klingelte. [Sie schlief bis zu dem Zeitpunkt, als es an der Tür klingelte.]

Zukunft mit *will* – *will-future*

Bildung
will + Grundform des Verbs

buy → will buy

Bildung von Fragen im *will-future*
(Fragewort) + *will* + Grundform des Verbs

What will you buy?
Was wirst du kaufen?

Bildung der Verneinung im *will-future*
won't + Grundform des Verbs

Why won't you come to the party?
Warum kommst du nicht zur Party?

Verwendung
Das *will-future* verwendet man, wenn ein Vorgang **in der Zukunft stattfinden** wird:
- bei Vorhersagen oder Vermutungen,

The weather will be fine tomorrow.
Das wird morgen schön.

I think she will take the red dress.
Ich denke, sie nimmt das rote Kleid.

- bei spontanen Entscheidungen.

Ok, I'll do that.
Ok, ich werde es machen.

Signalwörter: z. B. *tomorrow, next week, next Monday, next year, in three years, soon*

Zukunft mit *going to* – *going-to-future*

Bildung
am/is/are + *going to* + Grundform des Verbs

find → am/is/are going to find

Verwendung
Das *going-to-future* verwendet man u. a., wenn man ausdrücken will, was man für die Zukunft **plant** oder **zu tun beabsichtigt**.

I am going to work in England this summer.
Diesen Sommer werde ich in England arbeiten.

14 Liste wichtiger unregelmäßiger Verben – *list of irregular verbs*

Infinitiv	Präteritum	Partizip	Deutsch
be	was / were	been	*sein*
become	became	become	*werden*
begin	began	begun	*beginnen*
break	broke	broken	*brechen*
bring	brought	brought	*bringen*
buy	bought	bought	*kaufen*
catch	caught	caught	*fangen*
come	came	come	*kommen*
do	did	done	*tun*
drink	drank	drunk	*trinken*
drive	drove	driven	*fahren*
eat	ate	eaten	*essen*
fall	fell	fallen	*fallen*
feel	felt	felt	*fühlen*
find	found	found	*finden*
forget	forgot	forgotten	*vergessen*
get	got	got	*bekommen*

Infinitiv	Präteritum	Partizip	Deutsch
give	gave	given	*geben*
go	went	gone	*gehen*
have	had	had	*haben*
hear	heard	heard	*hören*
hit	hit	hit	*schlagen*
hold	held	held	*halten*
know	knew	known	*wissen*
leave	left	left	*verlassen*
let	let	let	*lassen*
make	made	made	*machen*
meet	met	met	*treffen*
pay	paid	paid	*bezahlen*
put	put	put	*stellen/setzen*
read	read	read	*lesen*
run	ran	run	*rennen*
say	said	said	*sagen*
see	saw	seen	*sehen*
sell	sold	sold	*verkaufen*
send	sent	sent	*schicken*
show	showed	shown	*zeigen*
sit	sat	sat	*sitzen*
sleep	slept	slept	*schlafen*
speak	spoke	spoken	*sprechen*
spend	spent	spent	*ausgeben/ verbringen*
stand	stood	stood	*stehen*
take	took	taken	*nehmen*
tell	told	told	*erzählen*
think	thought	thought	*denken*
win	won	won	*gewinnen*
write	wrote	written	*schreiben*

**Zentrale Prüfung am Ende der Klasse 10 – NRW –
Hauptschule Typ A / Gesamtschule GK – Englisch 2010**

Erster Prüfungsteil: Hörverstehen

Aufgabe 1: Selektives Verstehen: *Phone messages*

The Millers are not at home at the moment. You are going to hear some of the messages on their answering machine.

- *First read the example (0) and the sentences (1–5).*
- *Then listen to the messages.*
- *Complete the sentences while you are listening.*
- *At the end you will hear the messages again.*
- *Now read the example (0) and the sentences (1–5).*
  You have 30 seconds to do this.

Now listen to the messages and complete the sentences (1–5).

Example:

0. **The woman** tells John that Millie, the cat, is **next door**.

Message 1:

1. **Lucy** has forgotten the _____.

Message 2:

2. **Peter** asks Debbie to bring her _____ and the books.

Message 3:

3. **Renate** wants Mrs Hill to accept a _____ for her.

Message 4:

4. **Alice** wants to talk to Carmen because of the _____ on Saturday.

Message 5:

5. **Will** has a problem with his _____ for the party.

2010-1

Aufgabe 2: Detailliertes Verstehen: *How was your holiday?*

You are going to hear two conversations.
The people are talking about their holidays.

- First read the tasks (1–10).
- Then listen to the conversations.
- Tick the correct box for each task while you are listening.
- Tick only <u>one</u> box for each task.
- At the end you will hear the conversations again.
- Now read the tasks (1–10). You have 2 minutes to do this.

Now listen to the conversations and tick the correct box for each task (1–10).

Conversation 1

1. Simon …
   a) ☐ didn't like his holidays.
   b) ☐ loved his holidays.
   c) ☐ says the holidays were OK.

2. The skater park was …
   a) ☐ behind the shopping centre.
   b) ☐ in front of the shopping centre.
   c) ☐ near the shopping centre.

3. Simon went to the local takeaway and had Chinese food …
   a) ☐ every day.
   b) ☐ five times.
   c) ☐ quite often.

4. Julia …
   a) ☐ didn't like to be at home.
   b) ☐ liked to be at home.
   c) ☐ thinks it was terrible at home.

5. In her holidays Julia …
   a) ☐ did a lot of housework.
   b) ☐ read a lot.
   c) ☐ visited different museums.

Conversation 2

6. In her holidays Katie went …
   a) ☐ mountain biking.
   b) ☐ on an outdoor adventure trip.
   c) ☐ riding.

7. During the first part of the trip Katie …
   a) ☐ lost her rucksack.
   b) ☐ took a lot of pictures.
   c) ☐ walked through a waterfall.

8. Katie went skydiving. She …
   a) ☐ wasn't scared at all.
   b) ☐ was really scared at the beginning.
   c) ☐ was very scared all the time.

9. Katie jumped …
   a) ☐ in a group.
   b) ☐ on her own.
   c) ☐ with someone else.

10. In his holidays Ryan and his relatives …
    a) ☐ bought a new TV together.
    b) ☐ did a lot of sport outside.
    c) ☐ stayed in the house because of the weather.

Aufgabe 3: Globales Verstehen: *It drives me crazy*

You are going to hear 6 conversations. The people are talking about situations when someone is impolite.

- First look at the picture.
- Then listen to the conversations.
- You will hear each conversation twice.
- There is an <u>example</u> at the <u>beginning</u> (0).
- Write the numbers of the conversations (1–5) in the correct boxes in the picture.
- There is one more box than you need.
- Now look at the picture. You have 45 seconds to do this.

Now listen to the conversations and choose the correct box for each conversation (1–5).

Zweiter Prüfungsteil: Wortschatz – Leseverstehen – Schreiben

Aufgabe 4: Working in Australia – *The best job in the world?*

4.1 Wortschatz

4.1.1 Structure words

- Complete the following sentences with words from the box.
- Use each word only <u>once</u>.
- There is one more word than you need.

> too – when – after – later – because – that's why – first of all

1. _____ you are about 15 years old many parents start asking you what you would like to do after school.

2. But there are not only parents who try to help but teachers, _____.

3. _____ you have to find out what you like and what you are good at. Second you should be honest with yourself and find out what you don't like and what you are not really good at.

4. _____ that you should go to a job centre.

5. It's helpful to talk to a careers adviser[1], _____ he or she can give you detailed information about different jobs.

6. But then you still don't know what the job is really like. _____ many students do practical training in a company during their holidays for two or three weeks.

Annotation
1 careers adviser – *Berufsberater/Berufsberaterin*

4.1.2 Going on holiday to Australia

> Complete the following text with suitable[1] words.

Annotation
1 suitable – *passend*

Come to "Cooktown Paradise" – one of the nicest places in the very northeast of Australia.

1. Here in "Cooktown Paradise" there is a _____ climate all through the year. You only need some T-shirts and some shorts and sandals.

2. If you travel by _____ we pick you up from the airport.
3. You will find everything you need in our hotel. We offer a lot of outdoor _____, like cycling, walking and tennis.
4. For surfing, sailing and swimming we take you to our nice and sandy _____, which is only 400 metres from the hotel.
5. After an exciting day you can relax next to the pool. Our friendly _____ will be pleased to serve you with drinks and little snacks.
6. There is no problem if you don't speak fluent English. The people who work here also speak _____ like French, Spanish and German.

4.2 Leseverstehen: Working in Australia – *The best job in the world?*

After a worldwide search, Ben Southall was chosen as Tourism Queensland's Islands Caretaker[1], a job we like to call 'The best job in the world'. The job now is to help the Islands of the Great Barrier Reef to become more popular with tourists. His girlfriend Bridget is allowed to go with him. Here is what he says about the first days:

Read the paragraphs (0–5) and then do the tasks.

0. | G Example *Arrival in paradise* |

Wednesday 2nd July
The sound of my alarm clock woke me up from sleep and I got excited as I recognized that 'The best job in the world' starts here … Our arrival at Hamilton Island was great – I'm talking about a warm welcome from the staff of the holiday place. It really felt as if we'd finally arrived in paradise; the flight over the reef, the view as we came into land and then this – a really warm welcome.

1. | |

I loved the next part – showing my girlfriend Bridget our new home Blue Pearl – our new villa for the next six months. I showed her the three double rooms and of course the great balcony that looks over the Coral Sea. There will be lots of romantic evenings here. The welcome dinner was another great experience. If things go on like that I'll be the happiest man on the planet, the most tired man on the planet and maybe even the fattest man on the planet!

2. ☐

Wednesday 9th July
We're at Lizard Island now. The weather is fantastic: A clear blue sky with a few clouds and 28°C. The alarm clock finally woke me from sleep at 6 a.m., just in time for sunrise. With some other people I sailed out of the bay with a boat and into the open water to the reef. At this point the sea is 2 000 m deep! Here we jumped into the water and went diving.

3. ☐

We loved the warm water, which was about 26°C. A fantastic waterworld lay under us, with colourful corals as far as the eye could see. We saw barracudas, lionfish, parrotfish, the list just goes on and on. I can really say that I've never seen such a large number of different kinds of fish in one single dive.

4. ☐

Sunday 20th July
The usual busy days have gone for a while as Bridget and I finally have some days to relax back at Blue Pearl. First job on the list ... a visit to the dentist! I lost a tooth after I had tried to open a bottle with my mouth! So I had to see the doctor.

5. ☐

Tuesday 19th August
Today I visited the Club Med[2] at Lindeman Island. I had to play golf with a group of journalists from around Australia and New Zealand. I have played golf only once before. Not the best experience of my life! I also was afraid of being the only one who couldn't play golf. But hallelujah! Only one of us from the group of 20 had played in a golf club before so we were all absolute beginners. After all it was not my idea of a fun afternoon.

Annotations:
1 caretaker – *Hausmeister*
2 Club Med – holiday resort *(Urlaubsclubanlage)*

- *First read the headings (A–G).*
- *Then read the paragraphs (0–5) again.*
- *Find the right heading for each paragraph.*
- *Write the correct letters in the correct boxes.*
- *There is one more heading than you need.*

Headings

A	Paradise under water
B	Teeth problems
C	New activity, no fun
D	Making new friends
E	First boat trip
F	A luxury home
G	Example: *Arrival in paradise*

4.3 Schreiben

You have received an email from Kevin, your Australian pen friend.

- Read Kevin's email and write back to him.
- Answer <u>all</u> his questions. You can use ideas from the text "The best job in the world?".
- Think of a nice start and a nice ending to your email.
- Write complete sentences.

Hi ...,

Thanks for your mail. I'm sorry I took so long to answer it.

It's time for our summer holidays. My family and I are going to spend our holidays on an island near the Great Barrier Reef. There are lots of outside activities like diving, sailing and swimming. Have you already heard of Ben Southall and "The best job in the world"? He's a guy who is working for six months exploring the islands of the Great Barrier Reef. You must read his blog!

What do you think about his job?
Tell me what you like about it. Why?
Is there anything you don't like about it? Why not?

And what about *your* holidays this year – where are *you* going to spend the best time of the year? What are *you* going to do and who are *you* going to spend your holidays with?

Write back soon and let me know.

Best wishes,
Kevin

Lösungsvorschläge

Erster Prüfungsteil: Hörverstehen

Hauptschulabschluss Haupttermin
Wichtige Hinweise:
Alle Texte, die du im Folgenden hörst, werden zweimal vorgespielt. Vor dem ersten Hören hast du Zeit, dich mit den Aufgaben vertraut zu machen. Der Hörverstehenstest besteht aus drei Teilen:

Aufgabe 1: Selektives Verstehen: *Phone messages*

The Millers are not at home at the moment. You're going to hear some of the messages on their answering machine. First read the example 0 and the sentences 1 to 5. Then listen to the messages. Complete the sentences while you are listening. At the end you will hear the messages again.

Now read the example 0 and the sentences 1 to 5. You have 30 seconds to do this.

Now listen to the messages and complete the sentences 1 to 5.

Phone messages

This is 7589 67356. We can't take your call at the moment. Please leave a message after the tone.

Example

WOMAN: John, it's me. Listen, there's been an urgent problem ... I had to come into the office for a couple of hours. Anyway I've taken Millie next door. But can you fetch her and feed her? She'll be really hungry. And I won't be back before 7. Oh, you'll find her food under the sink, you know, in the cupboard there. I've written you a note about it too – it's on the fridge. See you later, OK? Bye!

Message 1

LUCY: Mandy? It's Lucy. Listen, I left the tickets on the kitchen table! Bring them with you! And can you get some sandwiches for the train? See you outside the station at 12, under the clock. Don't be late!

Message 2

PETER: Erm, Debbie, this is Peter. I'm sorry but I can't meet you at 12. How about a bit later, around 2? We can meet outside the library. Oh, and can you bring your laptop with you? And don't forget the library books. We have to return them today. See you later!

Message 3

RENATE: Hello Mrs Hill. It's Renate from next door. I'm going away next week and I'm expecting a parcel. I've tried to cancel but the store says it's on its way. Could you possibly take it in for me? If there's a problem, let me know.

Message 4

ALICE: Hi there, Carmen. It's me, Alice. Could you get back to me as soon as you can? It's about the trip on Saturday. It looks as if Michael and Jenny can't come after all and I was wondering if you knew anyone else who'd like to come. I think it's too late to get our money back. Anyway, talk to you later.

Message 5

WILL: Hi! It's Will. Listen, we have a big problem for the party tonight – my sound system is broken! Can you bring yours? Is that all right? And bring some dance music. Oh, and something to eat – crisps or something? Thanks. See you!

> *Now listen to the messages again and check your answers.*

Message 1
1. **Lucy** has forgotten the **tickets**.
    Hinweis: "... *Listen, I left the tickets on the kitchen table! ...*"

Message 2
2. **Peter** asks Debbie to bring her **laptop** and the books.
    Hinweis: "... *Oh, and can you bring your laptop with you? ...*"

Message 3
3. **Renate** wants Mrs Hill to accept a **parcel** for her.
    Hinweis: "... *I'm going away next week and I'm expecting a parcel. ... Could you possibly take it in for me? ...*"

Message 4
4. **Alice** wants to talk to Carmen because of the **trip** on Saturday.
    Hinweis: "... *It's about the trip on Saturday. ...*"

Message 5
5. **Will** has a problem with his **sound system** for the party.
   Hinweis: "... Listen, we have a big problem for the party tonight – my sound system is broken! ..."

Aufgabe 2: Detailliertes Verstehen: *How was your holiday?*

> You're going to hear two conversations. The people are talking about their holidays. First read the tasks (1 to 10). Then listen to the conversations.
> Tick the correct box for each task while you are listening.
> Tick only one box for each task. At the end you will hear the conversations again. Now read the tasks (1 to 10).
> You have two minutes to do this.
> Now listen to the conversations and tick the correct box for each task (1 to 10).

Conversation number 1

1   JULIA: Simon, good to see you. So, how was your holiday?
    SIMON: Oh, it was wonderful.
    JULIA: What did you do?
    SIMON: Well, let's see. I stayed at home. I did a lot of running in the early morning,
5   and I often went skateboarding with my friends.
    JULIA: Skateboarding? Oh, I didn't know you're a skater! Where did you do that?
    SIMON: There is this skater park just behind the shopping centre in King Street.
        We were lucky with the weather, so we could go there.
    JULIA: Ah, OK ... So what else did you do, Simon?
10 SIMON: Well, we also went to our local takeaway quite often. We got seafood and
        Chinese food three or four times!
    JULIA: Really?
    SIMON: Yes, shrimps, chop suey, great food and not expensive either. We enjoyed
        sitting together eating and talking. So how was your holiday, Julia?
15 JULIA: Well, I didn't go anywhere special, either. I wanted to, but I didn't.
    SIMON: So you just relaxed?
    JULIA: Yes, it was nice to be at home and have a lot of time for things like read-
        ing or listening to music. I did a lot of that. I probably read, I don't know,
        four or five thrillers. And I visited the new museum of sports. That was great;
20   you could see how the sports equipment has changed over the years. So it
        was relaxing and interesting, too.
    SIMON: Sounds nice.

1. b
   Hinweis: "Oh, it was wonderful." (Z. 2)

2. a
   Hinweis: "There is this skater park just behind the shopping centre in King Street." (Z. 7)

3. c
   Hinweis: "Well, we also went to our local takeaway quite often. We got seafood and Chinese food three or four times!" (Z. 10f.)

4. b
   Hinweis: "Yes, it was nice to be at home …" (Z. 17)

5. b
   Hinweis: "I did a lot of that. I probably read, I don't know, four or five thrillers." (Z. 18f.)

Conversation number 2

RYAN: Did you have a good holiday, Katie?
KATIE: Yes, it was exciting – probably my most exciting holiday ever.
RYAN: Wow! What did you do?
KATIE: I took a nature adventure tour. For the first part we went hiking. Phew, it was very tiring, but we had so much fun! We hiked all the way up to these beautiful waterfalls. I took lots of pictures. Have a look here.
RYAN: That looks great, Katie. So what else did you do on the tour?
KATIE: Well the best part was at the end of the trip. We went skydiving! Can you believe it? I jumped out of a plane.
RYAN: Wow! I would be too scared to do that!
KATIE: Well, at first I was really scared. The plane climbed to around 11,000 feet where I jumped out of the plane! Then I began to freefall. The dive lasted about five minutes!
RYAN: That sounds really dangerous. Were you alone?
KATIE: No, of course not. It was a tandem skydive. My instructor was very friendly.
RYAN: Wow!
KATIE: Yes, it was just a fantastic holiday. But anyway, that's enough about my holiday. How did you spend your holiday, Ryan?
RYAN: Oh, I visited my relatives.
KATIE: Uh–huh. Did you have a good time?
RYAN: Well, it was pretty boring, not like your holiday, Katie. It rained quite a lot, nearly every day, so we had to stay inside. We just stayed at home and watched TV a lot.

25 KATIE: Oh, that doesn't sound nice. Sorry to hear that, Ryan.
RYAN: It wasn't too bad. I mean it was relaxing, even though it was a bit boring.

> Now listen to the conversations again and check your answers.

6. b
   Hinweis: "I took a nature adventure tour." (Z. 4)

7. b
   Hinweis: "For the first part we went hiking. ... I took lots of pictures." (Z. 4 ff.)

8. b
   Hinweis: "Well, at first I was really scared." (Z. 11)

9. c
   Hinweis: "It was a tandem skydive." (Z. 15)

10. c
    Hinweis: "It rained quite a lot, nearly every day, so we had to stay inside." (Z. 22 f.)

Aufgabe 3: Globales Verstehen: *It drives me crazy*

> You're going to hear six conversations. The people are talking about situations when someone is impolite. First look at the picture. Then listen to the conversations. You'll hear each conversation twice.
> There is an example at the beginning (0).
> Write the numbers of the conversations (1 to 5) in the correct boxes in the picture. There is one more box than you need.
> Now look at the picture. You have 45 seconds to do this.
> Now listen to the conversations and choose the correct box for each conversation (1 to 5).

Hinweis: Die Stellen im Hörtext, die auf die jeweilige Situation im Bild hinweisen, sind fett markiert.

Example

MALE: I really don't like it. I mean why can't they **smoke their cigarettes** somewhere else? Some smokers just don't care about any sort of rules. They should know they're **not allowed to smoke in public buildings**. And even if they were allowed to do so they should think of the rest of the world.

FEMALE: You're absolutely right.

Conversation 1

FEMALE: I have a friend – a good guy – but **he's late all the time**. If he says we're going to meet at seven, he might get there by seven-thirty. I get so mad, especially when I'm waiting by myself somewhere. Sometimes I just want to leave and let him stand there alone.
MALE: Hmm. So – this also means, don't be late when I meet you.

> *Listen to conversation 1 again.*

Conversation 2

MALE: How about **people using mobile phones**? People use them everywhere now. I don't really mind if they use them outside in the street. I think it's OK in some places. But I'm just not sure about restaurants and cinemas and places like airports or stations. That seems very impolite to me.
FEMALE: Yeah. I feel the same way.

> *Listen to conversation 2 again.*

Conversation 3

FEMALE: Speaking of public places, I just don't understand it when **people throw their rubbish on the ground**. That makes many people so angry. I see people all the time eating sweets or snacks, and then they just take the paper and drop it. It's awful! I think they should pay a large fine.
MALE: Yeah. Or maybe the police should make those people go out and pick up all the rubbish. That would stop them.

> *Listen to conversation 3 again.*

Conversation 4

MALE: On my way to work this morning, I was waiting **in a queue** to buy an underground ticket. This **woman came up** and went right to the front of the queue. You should have seen **how angry some people got**. But I didn't care. I mean she was probably in a bigger hurry than me. I'm sure there was a reason why she couldn't wait. I guess I just don't mind waiting. I'm a very patient person.
FEMALE: I guess you are.

Listen to conversation 4 again.

Conversation 5

FEMALE: I'm always a little surprised when I see **an older person** standing somewhere, and **no one offers that person a place to sit**. You'll see young, healthy people just sitting there. I don't think it's very nice. I don't know. Maybe it's just me. When I was a young girl my parents told me to be polite to other people.

MALE: Yes, I think you're right. We should be more polite to older people.

Listen to conversation 5 again.

Ende des Hörverstehenstests

Zweiter Prüfungsteil: Wortschatz – Leseverstehen – Schreiben

Aufgabe 4

4.1 Wortschatz
4.1.1 Structure words

1. When
2. too
3. First of all
4. After
5. because
6. That's why

4.1.2 How to make money as a teenager

1. hot (warm, mild, moderate)
2. plane
3. activities
4. beach
5. staff (waiters, waitresses)
6. languages

4.2 Leseverstehen: Working in Australia – *The best job in the world?*

0. Arrival in paradise: G
   Hinweis: "... *It really felt as if we'd finally arrived in paradise; ...*"

1. A luxury home: F
   Hinweis: "... *our new villa for the next six months. I showed her the three double rooms and of course the great balcony that looks over the Coral Sea. ...*"

2. First boat trip: E
   Hinweis: "... *With some other people I sailed out of the bay with a boat ...*"

3. Paradise under water: A
   Hinweis: "... *A fantastic waterworld lay under us, with colourful corals as far as the eye could see. ...*"

4. Teeth problems: B
   Hinweis: "... *First job on the list ... a visit to the dentist! ...*"

5. New activity, no fun: C
   Hinweis: "... *I had to play golf... After all it was not my idea of a fun afternoon. ...*"

4.3 Schreiben

Hinweis: Bevor du anfängst, den Text zu schreiben, ist es wichtig, dass du dir die Arbeitsanweisungen sehr gut durchliest und diese einhältst.
Es ist keine Anzahl von Wörtern angegeben, die du schreiben sollst (z. B. Write at least 120 words). Vielmehr geht es nun darum, dass du alle Fragen, die in der E-mail zu finden sind, beantwortest. Dabei solltest du die Wortzahl trotzdem immer noch im Auge behalten, da ein zu knapper Text mit Sicherheit nicht alle Fragen, die in der E-mail gestellt werden, beantworten würde.

Hi Kevin,

Thanks for your mail, too. It's good to hear from you.
You asked me if I had already heard of Ben Southall and "The best job in the world?" Yes, I have. I have just read about him. His job is super. He lives in a villa with three double rooms and a great balcony that looks over the Coral Sea. And he goes diving in warm water, with a fantastic waterworld, colourful corals and barracudas. Who wouldn't like to work there? I would love to do his job.
The only thing that I don't like about the job is that Australia is so far away from Germany. I couldn't see my family and friends for a long time.
You asked me about my holidays this year. Well, I think I will stay at home. A holiday is too expensive for me at the moment. I will meet my friends and we will go out together or play with the computer.
Maybe I will visit my aunt in Oberhausen and then we will go shopping in a large shopping centre.

Please drop me a line when you have time.

Take care

(Your name) (193 words)

Zentrale Prüfung am Ende der Klasse 10 – NRW – Hauptschule Typ A / Gesamtschule GK – Englisch 2011

Erster Prüfungsteil: Hörverstehen

Aufgabe 1: Selektives Verstehen: *Big Ben*

You are going to hear a radio programme about Big Ben, one of England's most famous sights.

- *First read the example (0) and the sentences (1–5).*
- *Then listen to the radio programme.*
- *Complete the sentences while you are listening.*
- *At the end you will hear the radio programme again.*
- *Now read the example (0) and the sentences (1–5). You have 30 seconds to do this.*

© Claudio Divizia / Dreamstime.com

Now listen to the radio programme and complete the sentences.

Man:

Example:

0. The man tells the reporter that Big Ben is **150** years old.

1. The bells started ringing in _____, 1859.

Woman:

2. The woman says that Big Ben is the biggest bell in the _____.

3. Each bell has a _____ to make it ring.

Girl:

4. Climbing the tower is very hard. There are _____ steps to the top.

5. The _____ on the clocks are 60 centimetres high.

Aufgabe 2: Detailliertes Verstehen: *Living in a skyscraper*

You are going to hear an interview with Janet Ross. She is 23 years old and works as a secretary in Manhattan, New York. She lives in an apartment in a skyscraper.

© Image by Alfred Hutter

- First read the tasks (1–10).
- Then listen to the interview.
- Tick the correct box for each task while you are listening.
- Tick only <u>one</u> box for each task.
- At the end you will hear the interview again.
- Now read the tasks (1–10). You have 2 minutes to do this.

Now listen to the interview and tick the correct box for each task.

1. Janet Ross lives on the …
   a) ☐ 20th floor.
   b) ☐ 24th floor.
   c) ☐ 42nd floor.

2. Janet goes to work …
   a) ☐ by car.
   b) ☐ by bus.
   c) ☐ on foot.

3. Her apartment is …
   a) ☐ small and expensive.
   b) ☐ large and expensive.
   c) ☐ small and cheap.

4. The view from her apartment …
   a) ☐ could be better.
   b) ☐ is something she enjoys.
   c) ☐ is fantastic all the time.

5. Janet says that in most skyscrapers …
   a) ☐ you get to know people in the lift.
   b) ☐ you know the people from the lift really well.
   c) ☐ you always see the same people in the lift.

6. Janet explains that skyscrapers …
   a) ☐ are a place where families should live.
   b) ☐ usually have safe outdoor areas for children.
   c) ☐ sometimes offer family-friendly rooms and places.

7. Janet feels that the lifts …
   a) ☐ are not overcrowded.
   b) ☐ never work.
   c) ☐ often make you wait.

8. At night Janet …
   a) ☐ finds out first who's in the lift.
   b) ☐ waits for someone to check the lift.
   c) ☐ doesn't take the lift at all.

9. Asked where she would like to live, Janet …
   a) ☐ is undecided.
   b) ☐ knows what she wants.
   c) ☐ dreams of a garden.

10. Today living in a skyscraper is …
    a) ☐ becoming popular again.
    b) ☐ very safe.
    c) ☐ not liked very much.

Aufgabe 3: Globales Verstehen: *BBC World News*

You are going to hear the news of BBC World.
The reporter is talking about 6 different news items.

- *First read the headlines (A–G) and have a look at the list of the news items (0–5).*
- *Then listen to the news.*
- *Choose the correct headline for each news item and write the letters in the correct boxes.*
- *There is an <u>example</u> at the <u>beginning</u> (0).*
- *There is one more headline than you need.*
- *At the end you will hear the news again.*
- *Now look at the headlines (A–G). You have 20 seconds to do this.*

Now listen to the news and choose the correct headline for each news item.

	Headlines
A	Darkness helps wild animals
B	End of "Round the world record"
C	A visitor from the water
D	A dangerous workday
E	High tech examinations
F	Internet classrooms
G	Helpful millionaires (Example)

News items	Answers
News item 0 (Example)	G
News item 1	
News item 2	
News item 3	
News item 4	
News item 5	

Zweiter Prüfungsteil: Wortschatz – Leseverstehen – Schreiben

Aufgabe 4: *If your kids are awake*

4.1 Wortschatz

4.1.1 Structure words

- Complete the following text with words from the box.
- Use each word only <u>once</u>.
- There is one more word than you need.

> also – and – because – but – what – which – who

What makes a "smartphone" smart?

1. You have probably heard the term smartphone and wondered _____ exactly a smartphone is. You are not alone!

2. What is the difference between a smartphone _____ a "normal" cell phone? Why is a smartphone so smart?

3. Of course you can make phone calls with a smartphone. _____ you can use it for a lot of other things, too.

4. You can _____ do some things with it you usually do on a computer.

5. A smartphone is so smart _____ it can send and receive emails or other data and even create Office documents.

6. A lot of smartphones have a special keyboard _____ you can use to type messages as fast as on your computer.

4.1.2 The Internet

Complete the following text with suitable¹ words.

Annotation
1 suitable – *passend*

Good news for parents!

1. All those hours teenagers spend on the Internet are not a complete waste of _____.

2. The Internet can be a great place to visit. It can be fun, and you can keep in touch with _____ and chat with them.

3. Besides, it's fun to get and to write _____. It's a great way to tell others about yourself.

4. If a teen wants to find some _____ for a school project, the Internet is the first source.

5. This is why the Internet can be very useful and can help to improve your _____ at school.

6. In fact, many teens know far more about the wonders of the Internet than their _____.

4.2 Leseverstehen: *If your kids are awake, they are probably online*

A study shows that lots of young Americans use modern media in many ways.

Read the paragraphs (0–5) and then do the tasks.

0. | G Example *Two things at a time* |

Many teens today can multitask! They can do many things at the same time. For example, they surf the Internet while they listen to music. Because they can do two things at the same time one can say that they really spend nearly 11 hours using modern technologies in just seven and a half hours real time. "I feel my days would be boring without it," said Francisco Sepulveda, a 14-year-old teenager who uses his smartphone to surf the Web, watch videos, listen to music and send or receive about 500 text messages a day.

1. | _____ |

Dr. Michael Rich works at the *Children's Hospital* in Boston and he directs the *Center on Media and Child Health*. He says that the media are everywhere. "It's time to stop arguing over whether it is good or bad. Media are part of our children's environment, like the air they breathe, the water they drink and the food they eat." They grow up in a modern world where technological progress is something that they're interested in.

2. ☐

The bedrooms of America's children and teenagers are full of media. Nearly every young American has his or her own television, DVD player, computer or mp3-player. The list of modern technology that teenagers use every day is quite long. And the trend is that even more and more media find their place in young people's bedrooms. So teenagers can spend even more time watching, listening or playing. Computers already belong to the "old world". Almost one teenager out of three has his or her own laptop. Most young people can use a computer even if they don't have one of their own.

3. ☐

The study also shows that teenagers spend less time watching TV at regular hours a day. This is probably not very surprising because today there are many new ways to watch it: online viewing, films on iPods and even on mobile phones. This is also why the time spent watching TV has gone up from 3 hours and 51 minutes to 4 hours and 29 minutes per day. Everybody can even watch their favourite show after its real program time: the Internet makes it possible to watch a program 24 hours a day.

4. ☐

Only about three out of ten young people say they have rules on how much time they can spend watching TV (28 %) or playing video games (30 %). 36 % say the same about using the computer. Most of the time parents set these rules and their sons and daughters are not very happy with them. But can parents really know if they are watching a film or are playing a game? This is impossible because teenagers don't need a computer or a television set anymore to do this.

5. ☐

And no one can stop the digital revolution! Modern media use is developing at an unbelievable speed. Even during the study, it was changing. One of the hot topics today is Twitter which did not exist before teenagers were asked what role the media play in their lives. Computers, mobile phones and mp3-players become smaller, less expensive and multifunctional! And what's more, the batteries don't run low so quickly anymore.

(Zusammenstellung der Prüfungskommission, basierend auf: "If your kids are awake, they're probably online" by Tamar Lewin; New York Times, January 20, 2010)

- First read the headings (A–G). Then read the paragraphs (0–5) again.
- Find the right heading for each paragraph.
- Write the correct letters in the correct boxes.
- There is one more heading than you need.

Headings

A	Fast changes in technology	E	Too much media makes kids sick
B	Media at home	F	Modern ways of watching TV
C	Accept the facts	G	Example: *Two things at a time*
D	Parents and media control		

4.3 Schreiben

You have got an email from Gerry, your American pen friend from New York.

- Read Gerry's email and write back to him.
- Answer <u>all</u> his questions. The text you read before will help you!
- Think of a nice beginning and a nice ending to your email.
- Write 100 words or more
- Write complete sentences.

Hi ...,

Thanks for your email. I'm sorry I took so long to answer it. I was off-line for three days because my dad said I should stop for a while because I spent three whole days on the computer ☹. He wanted me to spend some time with the family! I almost went crazy ... without the Internet ☹.

What do you think about my father's decision[1]?

What rules do you and your friends have at home?

What electronic devices do you have or would you like to have? (cell phone, smartphone, mp3, iPod, TV, ...)

How often do you use them and what do you use them for? Or what would you like to use them for?

You see, I'm still a bit upset. This is why I'm asking all these questions.
Write back soon and let me know what you think about it.

Best wishes, Gerry

Annotation
1 decision – *Entscheidung*

Lösungsvorschläge

Erster Prüfungsteil: Hörverstehen

> Hauptschulabschluss Haupttermin
> Wichtige Hinweise:
> Alle Texte, die du im Folgenden hörst, werden zweimal vorgespielt. Vor dem ersten Hören hast du Zeit, dich mit den Aufgaben vertraut zu machen. Der Hörverstehenstest besteht aus drei Teilen:

Aufgabe 1: Selektives Verstehen: *Big Ben*

> You are going to hear a radio programme about Big Ben, one of England's most famous sights. First read the example (0) and the sentences (1–5). Then listen to the radio programme. Complete the sentences while you are listening. At the end you will hear the radio programme again. Now read the example (0) and the sentences (1–5). You have 30 seconds to do this.
>
> Now listen to the radio programme and complete the sentences.

1 REPORTER: Hello everybody! This is Jack Peterson speaking from London, right in front of Big Ben. Today I want to interview some people in order to find out what they know about this sight. But before we turn to the interview, listen to the world-famous sound of the bells.
5   Now, let's go! Excuse me, sir, could you please tell me what you know about our famous sight Big Ben?
    MAN: Erm ... let me think ... err ... Big Ben has just had its 150th birthday, I've just read that in the newspaper. The first clock started ticking on the 31st of May 1859, I believe, and some days later, on the 11th of July 1859, if I'm
10   correct, the bells rang for the first time.
    REPORTER: Thanks a lot, sir! ... Let's ask another person for more information on the bells ... Hello, Madam, erm, could you possibly help us out with the details on the bells of Big Ben?
    YOUNG WOMAN: You're lucky! I'm a tourist guide! So Big Ben, the largest bell
15   in the tower, is 2.2 metres high and 2.7 metres in diameter. But of course, it's not the only bell in the tower. There are four other bells. Now what's interesting about the bells is that normally bells move to ring, but not in this tower. They're fixed and there's a hammer on each bell, and the hammer hits the bell – and that makes the sound.

20 REPORTER: Wow, that's really interesting ... Thanks a lot! Now ... let's try our luck with one of our young Brits ... Excuse me, for our today's radio show, I'm looking for information on Big Ben. Can you help us?
STUDENT: Oh ... Am I on air now? ... Cool! Hi Mum and Dad, this is Janie. Ah – Everything is fine here in London! I, I've just visited the top of the tower.
25 It's 94 metres high ... but I can tell you, getting up there is better than one hour at the gym because you have to climb 334 steps. I remember that because I read about it for a school project, so I counted them to see if it's true – it is! And – you know what? The numbers on the clocks are 60 centimetres high! Can you believe that?
30 REPORTER: Thanks a lot for all that information! Now we all understand a bit better why Big Ben is Britain's most famous sight! You can read about all these facts on our local website ...

> Now listen to the radio programme again and check your answers.

Man
1. The bells started ringing in **July**, 1859.
   Hinweis: "... and some days later, on the 11th of July 1859, if I'm correct, the bells rang for the first time." (Z. 9f.)

Woman
2. The woman says that Big Ben is the biggest bell in the **tower**.
   Hinweis: "So Big Ben, the largest bell in the tower, is 2.2 metres high and 2.7 metres in diameter." (Z. 14f.)

3. Each bell has a **hammer** to make it ring.
   Hinweis: "... there's a hammer on each bell, and the hammer hits the bell – and that makes the sound." (Z. 18f.)

Girl
4. Climbing the tower is very hard. There are **334** steps to the top.
   Hinweis: "... but I can tell you, getting up there is better than one hour at the gym because you have to climb 334 steps." (Z. 25f.)

5. The **numbers** on the clocks are 60 centimetres high.
   Hinweis: "The numbers on the clocks are 60 centimetres high." (Z. 28f.)

Aufgabe 2: Detailliertes Verstehen: *Living in a skyscraper*

> You are going to hear an interview with Janet Ross. She is 23 years old and works as a secretary in Manhattan, New York. She lives in an apartment in a skyscraper.
>
> First read the tasks 1 to 10. Then listen to the interview. Tick the correct box for each task while you are listening. Tick only one box for each task. At the end you will hear the interview again. Now read the tasks 1 to 10. You have two minutes to do this.
>
> Now listen to the interview and tick the correct box for each task.

INTERVIEWER: Excuse me, Miss. I'm from Radio Five in London. We're doing a programme on "Life in great cities". May I ask you a few questions?

JANET ROSS: Yeah, sure, go ahead.

INTERVIEWER: You live in this skyscraper here. Right?

JANET ROSS: Yeah, it's got 42 storeys and I used to rent a flat on the 20th floor. It's been a while, however, since I've been living on the 24th floor.

INTERVIEWER: What's it like living in a skyscraper in Manhattan?

JANET ROSS: Well, one thing is really great. All the shops, theatres, restaurants, cinemas are close by. You can walk or take a bus. And the most important thing for me: I can walk to work.

INTERVIEWER: Have you got a car?

JANET ROSS: Oh no, I couldn't pay for a garage. People always think that flats in skyscrapers are inexpensive. My apartment, although it's pretty small, is terribly expensive. I wouldn't be able to afford a larger one.

INTERVIEWER: Do you have a good view from your apartment?

JANET ROSS: Mmmh-hmm. In fact, I do. You know the most impressive advantage of a flat in a skyscraper is the view. When you live on the 2nd or 3rd floor you usually see a house in the neighbourhood or, or a tree when you look through the window. Such a view can never be compared to the panorama through the window of a flat on the 24th floor. And – I really enjoy that fantastic view when the weather is fine.

INTERVIEWER: Do you know any of the people who live in your building?

JANET ROSS: Err, no, not really. In most skyscrapers you're quite lonely. You don't really get to know people in the elevator. You just stand there and you know, you see the same faces every day but you don't get to know them, which is really a pity. I think most people are aged between 20 and 30. But there are hardly any large families with children and no old people living in "my skyscraper".

INTERVIEWER: So, do you agree that families with children should not live in a skyscraper?

JANET ROSS: Yes, personally, I do agree, ... The fact is: One of the biggest disadvantages of most skyscrapers is ... they don't have separate yards for children to play in a safe and quiet atmosphere. And you can't send the children out to play, so to speak. And, besides, a really big apartment for a family in a "good" skyscraper with a lot of different community rooms to meet other kids ... like – in the swimming pool or in the sports facilities or in the garden ... would be terribly expensive. And then there is all the trouble with the elevators.

INTERVIEWER: What's that?

JANET ROSS: Well, you often have to wait for quite a while. Have you ever waited for an elevator for more than ten minutes?

INTERVIEWER: Well, no.

JANET ROSS: Well, I have, very often! You get fed up and angry because you want to catch a bus or get to work on time. Oh and then we had this problem with one of the elevators two years ago. It took them two weeks to repair it. It was terrible because the other elevators were even more crowded and you had to wait even longer. And sometimes I'm frightened, to tell you the truth.

INTERVIEWER: Frightened? Why?

JANET ROSS: When I ride the elevator alone late at night, for example, I'm always frightened that ... maybe someone could attack me. Lots of crimes happen at that time of the day and you wonder how many people still use it then. At night I always check who's in the elevator before I enter. And also if someone who's waiting with me makes me feel uncomfortable, I don't get on at all. Sometimes our caretaker checks on any strangers there, for safety reasons, you know.

INTERVIEWER: You said before you wouldn't like to have a family living in New York? Where would you like to live then?

JANET ROSS: Mmmh, I don't know, difficult to say. A house in the country would be wonderful, I guess. It must be much quieter. There is less traffic and you can have your own garden if you want to. I like flowers and trees but I wouldn't want to do all the garden work!

INTERVIEWER: Do you have some tips for someone who is looking for an apartment in a skyscraper in Manhattan?

JANET ROSS: Mmmh, well, for me personally safety is important. The construction of the block should be fire resistant and have modern sprayer systems, which is not always the case. A skyscraper also has to be safe when there are very strong winds and earthquakes. You know, it hasn't been popular to live or work in a skyscraper after September 11. But I feel that day by day this memory is slowly disappearing and living "in the sky" is becoming fashionable again and not disliked like it used to be shortly after September 11.

INTERVIEWER: Thanks for the interview. Good-bye.

JANET ROSS: Thank you. Have a good day.

> *Now listen to the interview again and check your answers.*

1. b
    Hinweis: "Yeah it's got 42 storeys and I used to rent a flat on the 20th floor. It's been a while, however, since I've been living on the 24th floor." (Z. 5f.)

2. c
    Hinweis: "And the most important thing for me: I can walk to work." (Z. 9f.)

3. a
    Hinweis: "My apartment, although it's pretty small, is terribly expensive." (Z. 13f.)

4. b
    Hinweis: "And – I really enjoy that fantastic view when the weather is fine." (Z. 20f.)

5. c
    Hinweis: "… in the elevator. You just stand there and you know, you see the same faces every day but you don't get to know them …" (Z. 24f.)

6. c
    Hinweis: "And, besides, a really big apartment for a family in a 'good' skyscraper with a lot of different community rooms to meet other kids … like – in the swimming pool or in the sports facilities or in the garden … would be terribly expensive." (Z. 34ff.)

7. c
    Hinweis: "Well, you often have to wait for quite a while." (Z. 39)

8. a
    Hinweis: "At night I always check who's in the elevator before I enter." (Z. 50f.)

9. a
    Hinweis: "Mmmh, I don't know, difficult to say." (Z. 57)

10. a
    Hinweis: "… and living 'in the sky' is becoming fashionable again and not disliked like it used to be shortly after September 11." (Z. 68f.)

Aufgabe 3: Globales Verstehen: *BBC World News*

> *You are going to hear the news of BBC World. The reporter is talking about 6 different news items. First read the headlines (A–G) and have a look at the list of the news items (0–5). Then listen to the news. Choose the correct headline for each news item and write the letters in the correct boxes. There is an example at the beginning (0). There is one more headline than you need. At the end you will hear the news again. Now look at the headlines (A–G). You have 20 seconds to do this.*
>
> *Now listen to the news and choose the correct headline for each news item.*

Hi there, I'm Sonali from BBC World News for young people. It's Wednesday, 9 June 2010. And this is the news for today.

0 Example
First to two of the richest men in the world: Bill Gates and the Mexican Carlos Slim want to give 150 million dollars to improve health systems in Mexico and Central America. Some of the money will be spent to fight serious illnesses like dengue fever and malaria – which can kill.

News item 1
And now imagine this. You're queuing up for lunch in the school canteen only to find out that a two-metre-long alligator has made its way into the hall. Some students in Florida could not believe their eyes when one appeared in their school. It seems the reptile escaped from a nearby river. Gary Moss, an official with Florida's fish and wildlife service, was called to the building to get the gator out of there.

News item 2
Next up – the story of one mechanic who got the shock of his life. Usually, when a car goes into the garage – the person working on it is on the look out for things that must be repaired. So imagine his surprise when a mechanic from London opened the bonnet of a van – only to find a snake on the engine! No one knows how it got there, but experts say it could be an escaped pet.

News item 3
Now forget uncomfortable classrooms – what would you think of taking tests in the comfort of your home? Well, a new computer programme has been developed that can let you sit exams at home – while making sure you don't cheat. It takes a fingerprint of the student to make sure that they are who they say they are. It also has a web-cam and microphone so that they can pick up on anyone else entering the room. And just to be extra sure – the programme blocks the Internet so that students can't search for answers.

News item 4

Just enough time for another of today's big stories – 16-year-old Abby who went missing when she tried to sail around the world has been found safe. Abby Sunderland's boat was caught up in massive storms in the Indian Ocean when she lost radio contact. Luckily, Abby was found by a rescue plane – but her boat's mast is broken so she's going to give up her plans.

News item 5

And finally – the New York skyline is one of the most famous in the world, but it's going to be a little harder to see in the dark for the next couple of months. Skyscrapers are switching off their lights at night to try and help birds. It seems that the light is distracting them and causes them to crash into buildings. Environmentalists hope that by turning off the lights, more birds will be able to fly to their destination safely.

Now listen to the news again and check your answers.

News item 1: Headline **C**
Hinweis: "... a two-metre-long alligator has made its way into the hall ... It seems the reptile escaped from a nearby river."

News item 2: Headline **D**
Hinweis: "So imagine his surprise when a mechanic from London opened the bonnet of a van – only to find a snake on the engine!"

News item 3: Headline **E**
Hinweis: "Well, a new computer programme has been developed that can let you sit exams at home – while making sure you don't cheat."

News item 4: Headline **B**
Hinweis: "... 16-year-old Abby who went missing when she tried to sail around the world has been found safe ... but her boat's mast is broken so she's going to give up her plans."

News item 5: Headline **A**
Hinweis: "Skyscrapers are switching off their lights at night to try and help birds."

Ende des Hörverstehenstests

Zweiter Prüfungsteil: Wortschatz – Leseverstehen – Schreiben

Aufgabe 4

4.1 Wortschatz
4.1.1 Structure words

1. what
2. and
3. But
4. also
5. because
6. which

4.1.2 The Internet

1. time
2. friends (people, your family)
3. emails (messages)
4. information
5. marks (grades)
6. parents (teachers)

4.2 Leseverstehen: *If your kids are awake, they are probably online*

1. C. Accept the facts
   ✎ *Hinweis:* "It's time to stop arguing over whether it is good or bad. Media are part of our children's environment, like the air they breathe, the water they drink and the food they eat."

2. B. Media at home
   ✎ *Hinweis:* "The bedrooms of America's children and teenagers are full of media."

3. F. Modern ways of watching TV
   ✎ *Hinweis:* "... today there are many new ways to watch it: online viewing, films on iPods and even on mobile phones."

4. D. Parents and media control
   ✎ *Hinweis:* "Most of the time parents set these rules and their sons and daughters are not very happy with them."

5. A. Fast changes in technology
   ✎ *Hinweis:* "Modern media use is developing at an unbelievable speed."

4.3 Schreiben

Hinweis: Wichtig ist, dass du dir die Aufgabenstellung und Gerrys E-mail genau durchliest, bevor du anfängst zu schreiben. Beantworte dabei <u>alle</u> Fragen, die Gerry dir in seiner Mail stellt. Denke auch an die Begrüßungs- und die Schlussformel. Deine Mail sollte mindestens 100 Wörter umfassen. Schreibe in ganzen Sätzen.

Hi Gerry,

Thank you for your e-mail. Oh dear, three days off-line is terrible! But your father's decision is right because it is important to spend some time with the family, too.

We've got some rules at home. My parents work all day. When they come home they check my homework. If I've done my homework, I'm allowed to watch TV for an hour or use the computer. One of my friends hasn't got any rules at home. He even sits at his computer at 3 o'clock in the morning. What do you think about that?

I've also got a mobile phone with which I call friends, take photos and listen to music, so I don't need my old mp3-player any more. I would like to have an iPod4 with a touchscreen. I could use the internet very easily and could get very good apps.

I've got my own computer, too. In the evening I play online games with my friends and I chat with them on facebook, but sometimes I also search for information for school.

Don't be upset. Spend some time with your family. It's ok.

Please write back soon.

Take care

(Your name) (194 words)

Zentrale Prüfung am Ende der Klasse 10 – NRW –
Hauptschule Typ A / Gesamtschule GK – Englisch 2012

Erster Prüfungsteil: Hörverstehen – Leseverstehen

Aufgabe 1: Hörverstehen Teil 1

Should teenagers stay in school until they are 18?
*You are going to hear a radio interview between **John Adams**, headmistress **Jean Collins** and 16-year-old **Stephen**. They are talking about the question of whether students should stay in school till the age of 18.*

- First read the tasks (1–6).
- Then listen to the interview.
- Tick the correct box or complete the sentences while you are listening.
- Tick only <u>one</u> box.
- At the end you will hear the interview again.
- Now read the tasks (1–6). You have 1 minute to do this.

Now listen to the interview and tick the correct box or complete the sentences.

1. The government is planning to raise the school leaving age by _____.

2. Stephen ...
   a) ☐ agrees with the government's plans.
   b) ☐ wants to stay at school till he's 18.
   c) ☐ will start working soon.

3. Ms Collins thinks that more students have better _____ when they stay at school longer.

4. Stephen says that a number of students would like to work ...
   a) ☐ in an office.
   b) ☐ with their hands.
   c) ☐ in school projects.

5. Stephen wants _____ to offer students more work experience to improve their skills.

6. Ms Collins and Stephen think of a _____ of school and work.

Aufgabe 2: Hörverstehen Teil 2

The Green Circle

*You are going to hear a radio interview between **Michael Mitchell** and **Jane Adams**, a tenth grade student.*

> - *First read the tasks (1–6).*
> - *Then listen to the interview.*
> - *Tick the correct box or complete the sentences while you are listening.*
> - *Tick only <u>one</u> box.*
> - *At the end you will hear the interview again.*
> - *Now read the tasks (1–6). You have 1 minute to do this.*

Now listen to the interview and tick the correct box or complete the sentences.

1. One day some school kids …
   a) ☐ started The Green Circle.
   b) ☐ read about The Green Circle.
   c) ☐ contacted The Green Circle.

2. After a discussion *The Green Circle* wanted to …
   a) ☐ save the whales.
   b) ☐ do something at their school.
   c) ☐ clean the rivers in their area.

3. *The Green Circle* got _____ from another environmental group.

4. The idea of a competition came from …
   a) ☐ a teacher.
   b) ☐ two girls.
   c) ☐ a boy.

5. Every _____ teachers give smileys to clean and tidy classes.

6. The project …
   a) ☐ will stop in two weeks' time.
   b) ☐ finishes after the end of the school year.
   c) ☐ will go on in the future.

Aufgabe 3: Leseverstehen

Absolutely normal chaos
by Sharon Creech (adapted)

Dear Mr Birkway,
Here it is: my summer journal. As you can see, I got a little carried away. The problem is – I don't want you to read it. I just wanted you to know I did it. I didn't want you to think I was one of those kids who say, "Oh yeah, I did it, but I lost it / my dog ate it / my little brother dropped it in the toilet." But please **Pleeeassse Don't Read it! I mean it.**
Sincerely,
Mary Lou Finney

Tuesday, June 12
I wish someone would tell me exactly what a "journal" is. When I asked my mother, she said, "Well, it's like a diary only different." Some help. She was going to tell me more, but Mrs Baker – our neighbour – came in. She was very angry because my brother Dennis had thrown eggs at her house. My mother flipped out and so she didn't finish telling me. How can I write a journal if I don't even know what one is? It's only because of Mrs Zollar, my English teacher. She asked us to write a journal this summer and give it to our new English teacher, Mr Birkway, after the holidays.
So, new English teacher, I'd better say, who I am. My name is Mary Lou Finney. I live at 4059 Buxton Road in Easton, Ohio. I have a normally strange family and here they are: let's take my pretty regular father first, Sam Finney. Most of the time he likes us, but sometimes we drive him crazy and then he goes out in the garden to pull out some weeds[1]. He is married to Sally, my wonderful mother, whose age I'm not allowed to tell anyone, not even my teacher.

Thursday, June 14
I still don't know how to write my journal but perhaps my seventeen-year-old sister Maggie can help me – if she wants to. You see, there is one problem. She is that kind of basic boy-crazy, fingernail-painting, annoying sister and the worst thing is I have to share a room with her. We often argue[2], but – you won't believe it – she has helped me!! (Sometimes she can be really nice ☺!) She told me to write down everything that comes to my mind … So, this journal is not as hard as I thought.

Monday, June 18
What's up for today? Nothing – just that I'm still not sure if this journal is really right. My sister told me, but, well – that's typically me – I'm still not quite sure and that reminds me of Alex Cheevey, one of my crazy classmates. When I wanted to ask my many questions about the journal, he said, "Geez. Can't you ever keep quiet? We don't want to know too much about this journal. We don't want to know how to write it. Then we'll have to do it right. So stop asking." And now I'm constantly thinking about his words …

Wednesday, June 20
So, dear teacher, that's my journal. I know it's not complete but I did my very best. And if you still don't know who I am, I can't help you 'cause I am waiting to find out, too.

---

1 weed – *Unkraut*

2 to argue – *streiten*

© *Sharon Creech: Absolutely normal chaos. London: Macmillan Children's Books UK 1990, p. 3–39*

Absolutely normal chaos

- *First read the text.*
- *Then do the tasks 1–6.*
- *For tasks 1, 2 and 5 decide if the sentences are true or false and tick the correct box. Then finish these sentences.*
- *For tasks 3 and 6 fill in the information.*
- *For task 4 tick the correct box. Tick only <u>one</u> box for this task.*

1. "Mary Lou wants her teacher to know that she has written her journal."
   This sentence is
   a) ☐ true   b) ☐ false

   because the text says

   _____

2. "Mary Lou's mother stopped talking about the journal."
   This sentence is
   a) ☐ true   b) ☐ false

   because the text says

   _____

3. Mary Lou has to write a journal because …

   _____

4. Mary Lou thinks her father is …
   a) ☐ quite pretty.
   b) ☐ usually normal.
   c) ☐ crazy.

5. "Mary Lou has got a room of her own."
   This sentence is
   a) ☐ true   b) ☐ false

   because the text says

   _____

6. How do you know that Alex Cheevy is not interested in the journal? Give two examples.
   a) _____

   b) _____

Zweiter Prüfungsteil: Wortschatz – Schreiben

Aufgabe 4: Wortschatz
4.1 A part-time job – Part 1

- Complete the following text (sentences 1–6) with words from the box.
- Use each word only <u>once</u>.
- There is one more word than you need.

| always | never | different | little | really | lots | some |

1. Every year _____ of students do a part-time job in their holidays.
2. But for _____ of them it's not easy to find the right job.
3. If you wait too long to look for one there is _____ chance to get the job you want.
4. The easiest way is to ask friends or to have a look at the ads in _____ newspapers.
5. Of course, it's _____ better to talk to your boss personally than just to contact him or her via email or phone.
6. Most students who have done a part-time job say that it's _____ important to know about the working conditions *before* you start a job.

4.2 A part-time job – Part 2

Complete the following text (sentences 1–6) with suitable[1] words.

Annotation
1 suitable – *passend*

1. Part-time jobs for students are quite _____ for companies and students.
2. And for both of them – companies and students – there are a lot of _____.
3. For the companies students are rather flexible and for the students it's a good _____ to get working experience and earn some money.
4. But before you _____ a job you should have a close look at the working hours.

5. There are students who like to _____ late in their holidays. So they should not choose a job that starts early in the morning.

6. Those who like to spend time with their friends at parties at the _____ should look for a job during the week.

Aufgabe 5: Schreiben

You got an email from Sam, your English pen friend from Manchester.

- Read Sam's email and write back to him.
- Answer <u>all</u> his questions.
- Think of a nice beginning and a nice ending to your email.
- Write 100 words or more.
- Write complete sentences.

Hi!
Thanks for your last email. I've got good news for us!!! You can come and stay with me and my family here in Manchester in the summer holidays ☺!!
Your idea to do a part-time job **together with me** here in Manchester is fantastic! My mum, dad and I asked nearly everybody here in town for a holiday job …
And guess what?! There are three jobs we could do together – isn't that great!
So let me know, what is really important for **you** in a part-time job?
Which **two** jobs are your favourite ones? Why?
Which job don't you like at all? And why not? (I hope it's not my favourite one!! ☺)
And here they are:

Job 1:
What: work in an ice-cream parlour
Earnings: £ 5 **per hour**
Working hours: Fri/Sat evenings from 6 pm – 9 pm

Job 2:
What: look after children (4 and 6 years old)
Earnings: £ 50 **a week**
Working hours: Mon – Thu from 7.30 am – 11.30 am

Job 3:
What: enter data into a computer (at home!!!)
Earnings: £ 75 **a week**
Working hours: depends on **you**!
(If you are very quick, you only need about 15 hours ☺!)

Pooh … really difficult!
Please write back quickly and let me know!
CU in Manchester soon,
Sam

Lösungsvorschläge

Erster Prüfungsteil: Hörverstehen – Leseverstehen

> *Hauptschulabschluss Haupttermin*
>
> *Wichtige Hinweise:*
> *Alle Texte, die im Folgenden zu hören sind, werden zweimal vorgespielt. Vor dem ersten Hören wird Zeit gegeben, sich mit den Aufgaben vertraut zu machen.*
> *Der Hörverstehenstest besteht aus zwei Teilen:*

Aufgabe 1: Hörverstehen Teil 1: *Should teenagers stay in school until they are 18?*

> *You are going to hear a radio interview between **John Adams**, headmistress **Jean Collins** and 16-year-old **Stephen**. They are talking about the question of whether students should stay in school till the age of 18.*
> *First read the tasks (1–6). Then listen to the interview. Tick the correct box or complete the sentences while you are listening. Tick only <u>one</u> box. At the end you will hear the interview again. Now read the tasks (1–6). You have 1 minute to do this.*
> *Now listen to the interview and tick the correct box or complete the sentences.*

1 JOHN ADAMS: Welcome to "What's up". My name is John Adams. Our topic today is the government's new plan to make teenagers go to school till they're 18. For our discussion I'd like to welcome 16-year-old Stephen from Stretford High School and Ms Jean Collins, a headmistress from Manchester.
5 MS COLLINS: Good morning, John.
STEPHEN: Hi, John.
JOHN ADAMS: Ms Collins, some politicians think too many young people leave school at the age of 16 without any qualifications. So the government is planning to raise the school leaving age from 16 to 18 by 2015.
10 MS COLLINS: Well, in my opinion, the age for students who leave school should be 18. You know, that's the age when they are old enough to be responsible for themselves.
STEPHEN: Sorry, Ms Collins, but ... I'm afraid I cannot agree with you here. There are also students who can take on responsibilities at the age of 16.
15 Look at me. I know what I want to do. I'm starting an apprenticeship next month. So why should I stay at school until I'm 18? I want to work and earn money.

JOHN ADAMS: I can see your point, Stephen. ... So, Ms Collins do you really think that the government should keep teenagers at school until they are 18?

MS COLLINS: Ha – well, you know ... I mean ... Don't get me wrong, Stephen. I don't want to say that students like you can't look after themselves at the age of 16. But the problem is that at the moment 11 % of the 16- to 18-year-olds don't do anything at all. They're not at school and they don't have a job. I personally think that raising the school leaving age to 18 can make sure that more young people have better skills and qualifications when they leave school.

STEPHEN: Ok, that's right. But you are talking about something that is only true for some students. Students are not all the same. They are different. Erm ... for example students who would like to do something practical – a work-based training or an apprenticeship maybe or even a full time job. – It would be better if they could find something so that they can work with their hands.

JOHN ADAMS: Do I understand you right, Stephen, you want politicians to work on projects in which young people could work and improve their skills but do not go to school any longer?

STEPHEN: Yeah, exactly. That would be much better for some of us. And I'm sure it would keep many young people off the streets.

JOHN ADAMS: Haha – that would be great! – Well, Ms Collins, what's your opinion on that?

MS COLLINS: That's a good point. I think our education system should be more flexible, more individual. I still think that young people under 18 need some kind of education or training. The question is: what exactly should students do at school till they are 18? Maybe we can have a combination.

STEPHEN: Yeah, that sounds interesting ... why not? You go to school and do something practical at the same time.

JOHN ADAMS: Maybe that is the right thing to do. – Well, this has been a very interesting discussion today. Ms Collins, Stephen, thank you so much.

MS COLLINS & STEPHEN: Thank you.

JOHN ADAMS: Join us again next week and get to know what other people think about ...

> Now listen to the interview again and check your answers.

1. The government is planning to raise the school leaving age by **2015**.
   Hinweis: "So the government is planning to raise the school leaving age from 16 to 18 by **2015**." (Z. 8f.)

2. c
   Hinweis: "I'm starting an apprenticeship next month." (Z. 15f.)

3. Ms Collins thinks that more students have better **skills (qualifications)** when they stay at school longer.
   Hinweis: "I personally think that raising the school leaving age to 18 can make sure that more young people have better skills and qualifications when they leave school." (Z. 23 ff.)

4. b
   Hinweis: "... for example students who would like to do something practical – ... so that they can work with their hands." (Z. 29 ff.)

5. Stephen wants **politicians** to offer students more work experience to improve their skills.
   Hinweis: JOHN ADAMS: "... Stephen, you want politicians to work on projects in which young people could work and improve their skills ..." (Z. 32 f.)
   STEPHEN: "Yeah, exactly." (Z. 35)

6. Ms Collins and Stephen think of a **combination** of school and work.
   Hinweis: MS COLLINS: "Maybe we can have a combination." (Z. 42)
   STEPHEN: "Yeah, that sounds interesting ... why not? You go to school and do something practical at the same time." (Z. 43 f.)

Aufgabe 2: Hörverstehen Teil 2: *The Green Circle*

> You are going to hear a radio interview between **Michael Mitchell** and **Jane Adams**, a tenth grade student.
> First read the tasks (1–6). Then listen to the interview. Tick the correct box or complete the sentences while you are listening. Tick only <u>one</u> box. At the end you will hear the interview again. Now read the tasks (1–6). You have 1 minute to do this.
> Now listen to the interview and tick the correct box or complete the sentences.

MICHAEL: Hello, this is Michael Mitchell speaking. In *Topics Today* I'd like to welcome Jane Adams from Parkside School in Bradford. Hello Jane, thanks for being with us today.
JANE: Hi, Michael, thank you for having me.
MICHAEL: Jane, you and your schoolmates have begun a special project at your school ... right?
JANE: Yes, we have.
MICHAEL: So, tell us, Jane ... what is it all about and how did it start?
JANE: Hmm, how did everything start? ... Well ... last year some of us read an interview about a green school in our area. – We really liked the idea of a

green school and wanted to do something similar! So we started a group called *The Green Circle*. We wanted to do something special for the environment. First we all thought about big things like saving the whales or fighting for clean rivers in our area.

MICHAEL: Haha, it sounds as if you wanted to save the whole world.

JANE: Haha ... absolutely! But then one of our teachers said, "Why always go big? Why don't you just start right here?" Well, after a lively discussion we realized that here at school we could actually do something, so our campaign "Fighting the rubbish" was born.

MICHAEL: I see. So – what was your next step, Jane?

JANE: Well ... before the project nobody really cared about rubbish and quite a number of students just dropped paper or plastic bags ... although we have rules. But many of the students just ignored them – a problem, of course.

MICHAEL: Oh yeah, I believe that.

JANE: So, what we did was the following: we went all around the school and collected all the rubbish. And – believe me – there was a lot! We looked through it and with the help of somebody from the local environment group we started to sort out the stuff in different boxes just like the City Council does. Then we put boxes for all the different kinds of waste in every classroom. The most difficult thing was to get the students to put the waste into the right boxes.

MICHAEL: And – did it work?

JANE: See, at the beginning it worked very well. But then – after some time – some of the kids just didn't care about their rubbish anymore.

MICHAEL: Sounds quite frustrating!

JANE: Yeah, we were really down. ... Two girls from grade 8 even left our group because they thought our project was useless and we had no idea how to change the situation. But then Thomas Parker from grade 9 suggested a competition.

MICHAEL: What kind of competition, Jane?

JANE: Well, the students of every class are responsible for a certain part of our school and, of course, for their own classroom. Those students who are best at keeping their area and classroom clean can win an extra day for a class trip! The teachers also like our idea and help us. Once a week they check the classrooms and those parts of the school ground their students are responsible for. If everything is OK, the students get a green smiley sticker. The class with the most stickers wins the competition!

MICHAEL: Oh, that sounds easy. Great! ... And, ah, who has the most stickers – the younger or the older ones?

JANE: Haha, well ... in two weeks' time, it will be the end of the school year – then we'll all know. And then: next year – a new chance for all of us!

MICHAEL: Great idea, Jane! ... – Thank you very much and all the best for your project.
JANE: Thank you, Michael.

> Now listen to the interview again and check your answers.

1. a
   Hinweis: "So we started a group called The Green Circle." (Z. 11f.)

2. b
   Hinweis: "Well, after a lively discussion we realized that here at school we could actually do something: ..." (Z. 17f.)

3. The Green Circle got **help** from another environmental group.
   Hinweis: "... with the help of somebody from the local environment group we started to sort out the stuff in different boxes ..." (Z. 27f.)

4. c
   Hinweis: "But then Thomas Parker from grade 9 suggested a competition." (Z. 38f.)

5. Every **week** teachers give smileys to clean and tidy classes.
   Hinweis: "The teachers also like our idea and help us. Once a week they check the classrooms and those parts of the school ground their students are responsible for. If everything is OK, the students get a green smiley sticker." (Z. 44ff.)

6. c
   Hinweis: "And then: next year – a new chance for all of us!" (Z. 51)

> Ende des Hörverstehenstests.

Aufgabe 3: Leseverstehen

1. true

   because the text says: *"Dear Mr Birkway, Here it is: my summer journal." (Z. 3 f.)*

2. true

   because the text says: *"She was going to tell me more, but ... she didn't finish telling me." (Z. 15 ff.)*

3. Mary Lou has to write a journal because **her English teacher, Mrs Zollar, wanted the class to write it**.

   ✏ **Hinweis:** *"It's only because of Mrs Zollar, my English teacher. She asked us to write a journal this summer ..." (Z. 23 ff.)*

4. b

   ✏ **Hinweis:** *"... let's take my pretty regular father first, Sam Finney." (Z. 32 f.)*

5. false

   because the text says: *"... and the worst thing is I have to share a room with her." (Z. 48 f.)*

6. a) *"We don't want to know too much about this journal." (Z. 65 ff.)*
   b) *"We don't want to know how to write it." (Z. 67 f.)*

Zweiter Prüfungsteil: Wortschatz – Schreiben

Aufgabe 4: Wortschatz

4.1 A part-time job – Part 1

✏ **Hinweis:** nicht verwendet: *never*

1. Every year **lots** of students do a part-time job in their holidays.
2. But for **some** of them it's not easy to find the right job.
3. If you wait too long to look for one there is **little** chance to get the job you want.
4. The easiest way is to ask friends or to have a look at the ads in **different** newspapers.
5. Of course, it's **always** better to talk to your boss personally than just to contact him or her via email or phone.

6. Most students who have done a part-time job say that it's **really** important to know about the working conditions *before* you start a job.

4.2 A part-time job – Part 2

1. Part-time jobs for students are quite **interesting** for companies and students.
2. And for both of them – companies and students – there are a lot of **advantages**.
3. For the companies students are rather flexible and for the students it's a good **chance** (**opportunity, idea**) to get working experience and earn some money.
4. But before you **choose** (**start, accept**) a job you should have a close look at the working hours.
5. There are students who like to **sleep** (**get up, stay up**) late in their holidays. So they should not choose a job that starts early in the morning.
6. Those who like to spend time with their friends at parties at the **weekend** should look for a job during the week.

Aufgabe 5: Schreiben

Hinweis: Wichtig ist, dass du dir die Aufgabenstellung und Sams E-Mail genau durchliest, bevor du anfängst zu schreiben. Beachte dabei folgende Punkte:
1. Beantworte alle Fragen, die Sam in seiner Mail dir stellt.
2. Finde einen passenden Anfang (Begrüßungsformel) und ein passendes Ende (Schlussformel).
3. Schreibe mindestens 100 Wörter.
4. Schreibe in ganzen Sätzen.

Hi Sam,

Thank you for your email and the good news that I can stay with you in Manchester in the summer holidays. I am really excited to meet you and your family and I am happy that you like my idea of doing a part-time job during my stay. Please thank your parents for asking so many people in your town for a holiday job for us. It is very good that you have found three jobs we can do together. For me it is important that I can earn some extra money. I need money for the trip to Manchester as it is expensive. I'll get some money from my parents, but I will have to pay for the rest myself. It is also great that both of us will get some work experience and that I can improve my English.

But now we have to decide which job is the right one for us. My favourite two jobs are working in an ice-cream parlour and entering data into a computer. If we worked in an ice-cream parlour we would meet a lot of new people and I could speak a lot of English. What is good is that the work starts at 6 pm, so we would be able to sleep late every day.

If we entered data into a computer we would work at your home and working with a computer wouldn't be new for us. That would also be a cool job.

I don't like looking after children, because we would have to get up very early. The job starts at 7:30 am! We would only get £50 for working a whole week with small children. This would probably be a hard job.

So, now you know my opinion about all three jobs. Please write back soon, because I would like to know what you think. Then we can decide which job we will choose.

I am really looking forward to my summer holidays in Manchester.

Take care
(Your name) (334 words)

> Zentrale Prüfung am Ende der Klasse 10 – NRW –
> Hauptschule Typ A / Gesamtschule GK – Englisch 2013

Erster Prüfungsteil: Hörverstehen – Leseverstehen

Aufgabe 1: Hörverstehen Teil 1

I am sailing

You are going to hear a radio discussion. **Ron** has invited **Jane** and **Tom**. They are talking about Laura Dekker, a Dutch teenager who sailed around the world on her own.

- First read the tasks (1–6).
- Then listen to the discussion.
- Tick the correct box or complete the sentences while you are listening.
- Tick only one box.
- At the end you will hear the interview again.
- Now read the tasks (1–6). You have 1 minute to do this.

Now listen to the discussion and tick the correct box or complete the sentences.

1. Ron …
   a) ☐ believes Laura is brave.
   b) ☐ thinks Laura is foolish.
   c) ☐ is not sure what to think about Laura.

2. When Laura started her trip she was …
   a) ☐ 13.
   b) ☐ 14.
   c) ☐ 15.

3. On her trip Laura didn't have enough time to _____.

4. Tom says that Laura was not old enough to understand all the _____
   _____.

5. Even two big organisations didn't accept Laura's _____.

6. Towards the end Jane …
   a) ☐ thinks Tom is right.
   b) ☐ disagrees with Tom.
   c) ☐ is becoming unsure about Laura's trip.

2013-1

Aufgabe 2: Hörverstehen Teil 2

Cool Job – Firefighter

*In the weekly high school podcast show "Job prospects", **Catherine Cox** is talking to **Stefan Gilbert**, a volunteer firefighter at Dallas County Fire and Rescue Station 13.*

- First read the tasks (1–6).
- Then listen to the podcast.
- Tick the correct box or complete the sentences while you are listening.
- Tick only <u>one</u> box.
- At the end you will hear the podcast again.
- Now read the tasks (1–6). You have <u>1 minute</u> to do this.

Now listen to the podcast and tick the correct box or complete the sentences.

1. Volunteer firefighting work is …
   a) ☐ during the week and on the weekend.
   b) ☐ on weekends only.
   c) ☐ only during the week.

2. To become a volunteer firefighter you must be good at _____.

3. The additional training for volunteer firefighters takes place …
   a) ☐ only once.
   b) ☐ each Saturday.
   c) ☐ every six months.

4. Stefan says that beginners can help the firefighters by …
   a) ☐ carrying water supplies.
   b) ☐ checking equipment.
   c) ☐ changing air-packs.

5. Firefighters know that fires are always put out by the whole _____.

6. To apply for the program you need a check-up from your doctor and from the _____.

Aufgabe 3: Leseverstehen

Facebook: The world's social network

There's a new name on the Forbes list[1] of the richest Americans. Mark Zuckerberg, only 26, the founder of Facebook, is already a billionaire.

Zuckerberg grew up in New York. He studied computer science, and it was during his studies that he and some friends had the idea of the social network site. In February 2004, together with fellow students, he organized Facebook from a room at the university.

At first Facebook was only for students at Harvard, but in March 2004, it had already been used in other universities. In June the same year, Facebook moved to Palo Alto, the California high-tech center. By December that year, the site already had nearly a million users. Today, Facebook is one of the most often visited sites on the Internet. By 2012, it had more than 800 million active users worldwide.

For many people, Facebook has become the way to keep in touch, share thoughts and photos, write messages and even find old friends they had lost contact with. The average Facebook user has 130 Facebook friends – some are family and friends, but others are people they don't have time to see very often.

Richard Allan, who runs Facebook Europe says: "In real life, you have enough time to regularly go out with 20 to 30 people. With Facebook your social circle grows by another 100 people."

But is social networking one of the best things that happened to the Internet? Not everyone is sure. There has been criticism of the way personal information can become public. Facebook has so-called "privacy settings" which means that the user can decide who is allowed to see all the private information. However, some users found the settings too difficult and it took too much time to install them. So they didn't use them and gave away information they wanted to keep private.

In 2010 Mark Zuckerberg had his own privacy problem: a film, "The Social Network", tells the story of how Facebook was founded – and gives a rather negative picture of Zuckerberg. The film shows him as a very intelligent computer freak who doesn't even care about the friends who helped to start Facebook.

The film starts with him being left by his girlfriend. He then goes on a journey where he shows arrogance and social envy[2] on his way to becoming a billionaire. In the movie Zuckerberg's motivation to build Facebook was to impress a girl and get social acceptance. "That's false", says David Kirkpatrick, who wrote a book about Zuckerberg and the beginning of Facebook. "Actually Zuckerberg is not arrogant. His motivation was to come up with a new way to share information on the Internet", he says. "The film is only 40 % true."

Zuckerberg's statement about the film was simply: "It's a movie. It's fun. A lot of it is not real."

---

1 Forbes list – *jährlich veröffentlichte Liste des Forbes Magazine* The World's Billionaires

2 envy – *Neid*

- *First read the text.*
- *Then do the tasks 1–6.*
- *For tasks 1, 4 and 5 decide if the sentences are true or false and tick the correct box. Then finish these sentences.*
- *For task 3 fill in the information.*
- *For tasks 2 and 6 tick the correct box. Tick only one box for this task.*

1. At the beginning, Facebook was for Harvard students only.
   This sentence is

   a) ☐ true   b) ☐ false

   because the text says

   _____

2. The text says that Facebook gives people the chance to have …
   a) ☐ 100
   b) ☐ 130
   c) ☐ 20–30
   more friends than usual.

3. Not everybody uses the possibilities to keep private. Give two reasons.
   a) _____
   b) _____

4. The film "The Social Network" presents Zuckerberg as a helpful friend.
   This sentence is

   a) ☐ true   b) ☐ false

   because the text says

   _____

5. David Kirkpatrick says that Zuckerberg started Facebook because he wanted to find a girlfriend.
   This sentence is

   a) ☐ true   b) ☐ false

   because the text says

   _____

6. In the end Zuckerberg says the film …
   a) ☐ is too simple.
   b) ☐ makes fun of him.
   c) ☐ is only partly true.

Zweiter Prüfungsteil: Wortschatz – Schreiben

Aufgabe 4: Wortschatz – *Into the world of work*
4.1 Getting a job – Part 1

- Complete the following text with words from the box.
- Use each word only <u>once</u>.
- There is one more word than you need.

| also | already | most | enough | always | without | if |

1. Getting a job is one of the _____ important things for young people.
2. But it is not _____ easy to find the right job.
3. Of course, earning _____ money in a job is very important.
4. You cannot live _____ money.
5. But it is _____ very important that you like your job.
6. It can make you very unhappy _____ you hate your job.

4.2 Job interviews – Part 2

Complete the following text (sentences 1–6) with suitable words.

Here are some rules for job interviews:

1. You should _____ on time.
2. You should wear the right _____.
3. Remember to _____ your mobile before you enter the room.
4. Don't be too nervous, so try to be as _____ as possible.
5. Be polite and _____ all the time.
6. And it is very important to know what to say when you are asked why you _____ the job.

Aufgabe 5: Schreiben

You got an email from your American email friend Norman.

- Read Norman's email and write back to him.
- Answer <u>all</u> his questions.
- Think of a nice beginning and a nice ending to your email.
- Write <u>100 words</u> or more.
- Write an email with <u>complete sentences</u>.

Hi!

Sorry for my late answer! Just too much to do!

I've just finished my work placement[1] at the restaurant of the Hilton Hotel here in Chicago. It was just awesome! All my colleagues were very nice. Of course, sometimes it was also quite stressful. But you feel great when you hear that people liked what you cooked! I think it's the right kind of job for me – although it means working on weekends and in the evenings.

But the problem is one of the trainee cooks told me you need to be good at math to become a cook. Maybe he's right. Recipes are full of numbers! And, to be honest, math is not my best subject … Well – I'll try and find out more about it. – What about you?

What work experience do **you** have? How did it help **you** to find the kind of job you want to do?

What job would **you** like to do and why?

What skills or qualifications do you need for the job?

What would you hate in a job? Why?

OK – I must go now. You know, I've got a Saturday job at a supermarket …

Take care,

Norman

---

1 work placement – a period of work experience

Lösungsvorschläge

Erster Prüfungsteil: Hörverstehen – Leseverstehen

Hauptschulabschluss Haupttermin

Wichtige Hinweise:
Alle Texte, die im Folgenden zu hören sind, werden zweimal vorgespielt. Vor dem ersten Hören wird Zeit gegeben, sich mit den Aufgaben vertraut zu machen. Der Hörverstehenstest besteht aus zwei Teilen:

Aufgabe 1: Hörverstehen Teil 1: *I am sailing*

You are going to hear a radio discussion. Ron has invited Jane and Tom. First read the tasks (1–6). Then listen to the discussion. Tick the correct box or complete the sentences while you are listening. Tick only <u>one</u> box. At the end you will hear the discussion again. Now read the tasks (1–6). You have 1 minute to do this.

Now listen to the discussion and tick the correct box or complete the sentences.

1 RON: And here we are again for this week's *Who has the best arguments?* – I'd like to welcome Jane and Tom from Peterborough to our discussion.
   JANE: Hi Ron, nice to be here.
   TOM: Hi – thanks for inviting me.
5 RON: Today we're gonna talk about the Dutch girl Laura Dekker who became the youngest person to sail solo around the world in 2012 – all alone on her sailing boat called "Guppy". For many people she's brave, for others she's just foolish. – Personally, I don't really know what to think of her idea.
   TOM: Well, Ron, let me tell you what I think. She actually wanted to do the jour-
10   ney much earlier, in 2009 when she was 13. But the Dutch government stopped her. They said she was far too young. When she finally started on 21st August 2010 she was not even 15. And I think – even then – she was still too young.
   JANE: Well ... it sounds right what you say Tom, but you forget that she comes
15   from a sailing family and has *lots* of experience. So, ... I think it was ... under certain conditions ... OK.
   RON: Which conditions?
   JANE: Well – the journey was well planned and her team did everything to make sure it was safe.

TOM: Are you joking, Jane? Just imagine the dangers at sea, not enough sleep and being alone all the time. And – she didn't learn much for school while she was at sea – you know? Full time education is a must in the Netherlands until you are 16 ... And, honestly ... can you see her going back to the classroom after this?

JANE: Ha – ha ... ah ... not really, no ... but ... erm ... I mean she seems to be like a 20-year-old woman.

TOM: Yes, but look, she isn't an adult, Jane. She isn't even allowed to drive a car. She was still too young to understand the dangers completely. From time to time she had to stop her 50,000 km journey because of heavy winds and high seas. And ... she didn't always have access to the Internet – to get help, for example.

JANE: Well, I read that there were moments when Laura asked herself if what she was doing was right. This shows that she knew the dangers. But the experience she had on that journey is more than most people have in their lifetime.

TOM: Definitely no doubt about that – but just imagine if something had happened to her. See, all those people who were against the trip only had her safety in mind. Even the World Sailing Federation and Guinness World Records didn't accept her world record. They don't want teenagers to follow Laura's idea. Don't you think it would be just as great if she was just a few years older?

JANE: Hm ... well, you might be right about that, Tom.

RON: So, has he finally convinced you, Jane?

JANE: Ha. Well, Tom, I'm ... well, I'm not sure ... I can follow you somehow, but ... you see ... just give me some time to think about it.

RON: OK, so what do you, the listeners, think? Who has been more convincing – Jane or Tom? Was Laura a brave young girl, or just careless? ...

> Now listen to the discussion again and check your answers.

1. c
   ✏ *Hinweis:* "Personally, I don't really know what to think of her idea." (Z. 8)

2. b
   ✏ *Hinweis:* "When she finally started on 21st August 2010 she was not even 15." (Z. 11 f.)

3. On her trip Laura didn't have enough time to **sleep/learn**.
   ✏ *Hinweis:* "Just imagine the dangers at sea, not enough sleep and being alone all the time. And – she didn't learn much for school while she was at sea – you know?" (Z. 20 ff.)

4. Tom says that Laura was not old enough to understand all the **dangers**.
   Hinweis: "She was still too young to understand the dangers completely." (Z. 28)

5. Even two big organisations didn't accept Laura's **record/world record**.
   Hinweis: "Even the World Sailing Federation and Guinness World Records didn't accept her world record." (Z. 37f.)

6. c
   Hinweis: "Ha. Well, Tom, I'm ... well, I'm not sure ... I can follow you somehow, but ..." (Z. 43f.)

Aufgabe 2: Hörverstehen Teil 2: *Cool Job – Firefighter*

> *In the weekly high school podcast show "Job prospects", Catherine Cox is talking to Stefan Gilbert, a volunteer firefighter at Dallas County Fire and Rescue Station 13.*
>
> *First read the tasks (1–6). Then listen to the podcast. Tick the correct box or complete the sentences while you are listening. Tick only <u>one</u> box. At the end you will hear the podcast again. Now read the tasks (1–6). You have 1 minute to do this.*
>
> *Now listen to the podcast and tick the correct box or complete the sentences.*

1 CATHERINE: Saturday night, 11 pm. You're sleeping. Suddenly a loud bell rings, a red light flashes. Everybody jumps out of bed. – This is the everyday business of Stefan Gilbert, a volunteer firefighter at Dallas County Fire and Rescue Station 13. Stefan, welcome to our weekly show "Job prospects", our high
5 school podcast.
   STEFAN: Thanks very much, Catherine. Nice to be here today!
   CATHERINE: And welcome to all our listeners. Well, now, you guys out there – you like to help people. You like to test your skills in extreme situations. Ha, then Stefan's job might be the right job for you! Stefan, could you tell us a little
10 bit more about it?
   STEFAN: Yes, sure! During the week, you live your normal life like every other teenager. But on weekends, from Saturday, 10 am, until Sunday, 9 pm, you turn into a real hero. You not only save a cat that can't climb down a tree. You also help people who are in danger because a storm damaged their home,
15 or you even get the chance to save people's lives in a fire.
   CATHERINE: Wow – that sounds really dangerous. – Can anybody become a volunteer firefighter?
   STEFAN: Well, anybody from the age of 16. The only condition is that you are good at school and your average grades must be at least 2.0. – Just come to

our special classes. For half a year, we'll teach you everything about our job on two nights a week from 7:00 to 10:30 pm.

CATHERINE: That's all?

STEFAN: Haha, no, haha – of course not. Fighting fires is dangerous. So, continuous training is important! That's why you have to attend additional training with our experts each Saturday during these six months. – And once you've learned all the things you need to stay safe whatever might happen, you step into the danger zone.

CATHERINE: Wow!

STEFAN: You're a real volunteer firefighter now!

CATHERINE: That sounds like a long way to go ...

STEFAN: Don't worry! – You can be at emergency sites right from the start. There's a lot of work to do: you can help the other firefighters by checking the water supply, or carrying equipment and changing air-packs.

CATHERINE: So you need to be a team player to be a volunteer firefighter?

STEFAN: Oh yes, always remember: it's the whole team that puts the fire out!

CATHERINE: That sounds great! And how can someone like us join your program?

STEFAN: Here's what you've got to do: First: fill out the application form and get your parents' permission. Second: go to your doctor! You must be really fit and healthy, so ask your doctor for a medical check. And finally: go to the nearest police department and get a police background check, that's a paper that proves that you're not a criminal. Got everything? – Then go ahead! And always remember: we want you – hahaha!

> Now listen to the podcast again and check your answers.

1. b
   Hinweis: "But on weekends, from Saturday, 10 am, until Sunday, 9 pm, you turn into a real hero." (Z. 12 f.)

2. To become a volunteer firefighter you must be good at **school**.
   Hinweis: "The only condition is that you are good at school ..." (Z. 18 f.)

3. b
   Hinweis: "That's why you have to attend additional training with our experts each Saturday during these six months." (Z. 24 f.)

4. c
   Hinweis: "There's a lot of work to do: you can help the other firefighters by checking the water supply, or carrying equipment and changing air-packs." (Z. 32 f.)

5. Firefighters know that fires are always put out by the whole **team**.
   ✐ *Hinweis:* "Oh yes, always remember: it's the whole team that puts the fire out!" (Z. 35)

6. To apply for the program you need a check-up from your doctor and from the **police (department)**.
   ✐ *Hinweis:* "And finally: go to the nearest police department and get a police background check ..." (Z. 40 f.)

Ende des Hörverstehenstests.

Aufgabe 3: Leseverstehen

1. true
   because the text says "At first Facebook was only for students at Harvard ..." (Z. 13 f.)

2. a
   ✐ *Hinweis:* "With Facebook your social circle grows by another 100 people." (Z. 36 f.)

3. a) Some users found the settings too difficult. (Z. 46 f.)
   b) It took too much time to install them. (Z. 47 f.)

4. false
   because the text says "... the story ... gives a rather negative picture of Zuckerberg" (Z. 53 ff.); or:
   "... [he] doesn't even care about the friends who helped to start Facebook." (Z. 57 ff.); or:
   "He ... shows arrogance and social envy ..." (Z. 62 f.)

5. false
   because the text says " 'Actually Zuckerberg is not arrogant. His motivation was to come up with a new way to share information on the Internet.' " (Z. 69 ff.)

6. c
   ✐ *Hinweis:* "It's a movie. It's fun. A lot of it is not real." (Z. 76 f.)

Zweiter Prüfungsteil: Wortschatz – Schreiben

Aufgabe 4: Wortschatz – *Into the world of work*

4.1 Getting a job – Part 1

✐ **Hinweis:** Nicht benutzt: *already*

1. Getting a job is one of the **most** important things for young people.
2. But it is not **always** easy to find the right job.
3. Of course, earning **enough** money in a job is very important.
4. You cannot live **without** money.
5. But it is **also** very important that you like your job.
6. It can make you very unhappy **if** you hate your job.

4.2 Job interviews – Part 2

1. You should **arrive/be** (**right**) on time.
2. You should wear the right **clothes/outfit**.
3. Remember to **turn off/switch off** your mobile before you enter the room.
4. Don't be too nervous, so try to be as **relaxed / natural / calm / normal / self-confident** as possible.
5. Be polite and **friendly/listen/pay attention** all the time.
6. And it is very important to know what to say when you are asked why you **are interested in/applied for/want** (**to get/to have/to do**) the job.

Aufgabe 5: Schreiben

✐ **Hinweis:** *Lies dir die Aufgabenstellung und Normans E-Mail genau durch, bevor du anfängst zu schreiben. Beachte dabei folgende Punkte:*
1. *Beantworte alle Fragen, die dir Norman in seiner Mail stellt.*
2. *Finde einen passenden Anfang (Begrüßungsformel) und ein passendes Ende (Schlussformel).*
3. *Schreibe mindestens 100 Wörter.*
4. *Schreibe in ganzen Sätzen.*

Dear Norman,

Don't worry about being late with your answer. It's just the same for me. I have to work a lot too.

Your work placement at the restaurant in the Hilton Hotel must have been a very special experience. Did you also meet a lot of rich and famous people? I could also imagine myself working in a hotel.

Some weeks ago I finished my work placement as a car mechanic at our local garage. I really liked it there and, when I leave school, I could start an apprenticeship at the garage. I love cars and I am looking forward to getting my driving licence. I help my older brother to repair and clean his car. Recently, I have helped him tune up the engine of his car. So I have already some of the experience and skills that you need for the job.

What I would hate in a job is working hard for hardly any money. You work the whole day, but you can't keep a family or enjoy life.

That's all for now. I'm going out with my friends tonight. Don't work too much and have some fun too!

Take care,

(Your name)

(196 words)

**Zentrale Prüfung am Ende der Klasse 10 – NRW –
Hauptschule Typ A / Gesamtschule GK – Englisch 2014**

Erster Prüfungsteil: Hörverstehen – Leseverstehen

Aufgabe 1: Hörverstehen Teil 1

The Tube

*The London Underground plays a big part in the lives of Londoners. In 2013 the London Underground celebrated its 150th birthday. Listen to **Jackie** and **Richard** from Urban News.*

- First read the tasks (1–6).
- Then listen to the programme.
- Tick the correct box or complete the sentences while you are listening.
- Tick only <u>one</u> box.
- At the end you will hear the programme again.
- Now read the tasks (1–6). You have <u>1 minute</u> to do this.

Now listen to the programme and do the tasks.

1. In 1863 the London Tube started with …
   a) ☐ the Farringdon Line.
   b) ☐ the Paddington Line.
   c) ☐ the Metropolitan Line.

2. Workers had to dig tunnels under the city _____.

3. Steam trains on the underground …
   a) ☐ used wood fires.
   b) ☐ made it difficult to breathe.
   c) ☐ were only used in the 19th century.

4. When the city was being bombed in the Second World War Londoners _____ in the tunnels.

5. After a fire King's Cross Station …
   a) ☐ lost its popularity.
   b) ☐ became a tourist sight.
   c) ☐ was closed for some time.

2014-1

6. Tip for tourists:
   a) ☐ Mind the famous warning.
   b) ☐ The Tube map is like a street map.
   c) ☐ The underground map shows reality.

Aufgabe 2: Hörverstehen Teil 2

McDonald's

You are going to hear a radio program called 'Success Stories in the USA'.
Lynn McCain *and* ***Anthony Johnson*** *are talking about the history of McDonald's restaurants.*

- First read the tasks (1–6).
- Then listen to the program.
- Tick the correct box or complete the sentences while you are listening.
- Tick only <u>one</u> box.
- At the end you will hear the program again.
- Now read the tasks (1–6). You have <u>1 minute</u> to do this.

Now listen to the program and do the tasks.

1. McDonald's will soon celebrate its _____ th birthday.

2. From 1948 …
   a) ☐ professional cooks made the food.
   b) ☐ the menu was much longer than before.
   c) ☐ the San Bernadino restaurant had self-service.

3. In 1954, Richard and Maurice McDonald …
   a) ☐ sold their business idea.
   b) ☐ opened restaurants all over the US.
   c) ☐ changed the style of their restaurants.

4. The first European McDonald's was opened in …
   a) ☐ Britain.
   b) ☐ Germany.
   c) ☐ the Netherlands.

5. Worldwide, around _____ million people **work** for McDonald's.

6. Restaurants in New York called the meat in the burgers _____.

Aufgabe 3: Leseverstehen

Shrovetide[1] Football – a crazy ball game

A *Ashbourne Royal Shrovetide Football* is a crazy ball game for young and old that is more than 1,000 years old. It is played in the little town of Ashbourne. Although it is called 'football' it is nothing like a standard football game. – But what makes *Ashbourne Royal Shrovetide Football* – one of Britain's oldest sports – so special? Well, there are many things.

B Strangely enough the ball is filled with cork and it is bigger and heavier than a standard football. What makes the ball unique is that it is hand-painted with a new design every year. It takes about a month to paint the ball. So you can imagine that they even have guards to prevent[2] souvenir-hunters from stealing the ball.

C The game is on Shrove Tuesday and Ash Wednesday[3]. It starts at 2 pm and has to finish by 10 pm on each day. If a player can score a goal before 5 pm on the first day, a new ball is thrown in and the match starts again. If a player scores a goal after 5 pm, the match ends on that day and starts again on the second and final day at 2 pm.

D About 400 people, mostly from Ashbourne, take part. They are divided into two teams called the Up'ards and the Down'ards. Why is that? Well, Henmore River flows through the town and splits the city into two parts – and two teams. The players who were born north of Henmore River are the Up'ards. They must take the ball to a small stone wall near the river east of the town. The players who were born south of Henmore River are called the Down'ards. They must take the ball to a small stone wall near the river west of the town – three miles away from the stone wall in the east.

E And believe it or not – the game is played in the streets, in the fields and even in the river. As there is no referee you could think that the game always ends in fights. But this is not the case because there are things the players have to accept: they must keep out of other people's gardens and public parks. The ball can be thrown, kicked or carried. But it must not be hidden or transported in a motor vehicle and the players have to play fair.

F Of course there is a lot of preparation in the weeks before Shrovetide. Some of the players train to be runners; others train as 'river specialists'. This is because the ball may fall into Henmore River. And – the player who wants to score a goal has to stand in Henmore River and throw the ball three times against the small stone wall which serves as the goal. The 'river specialists' wear special clothes because it gets cold in the river in February!

G When a player has scored a goal he is carried back into the town on the team-players' shoulders and cheered by hundreds of tourists. And he gets the hand-painted ball as a prize. Well, one thing is certain: *Ashbourne Royal Shrovetide Football* is a very unusual game but it is a lot of fun – for the players and for the people who watch the match.

---

1 Shrovetide – *Karneval, Fasching*
2 to prevent sb from doing sth – *jdn. hindern etwas zu tun*
3 Shrove Tuesday and Ash Wednesday – *Karnevalsdienstag und Aschermittwoch*

Task 1

- *First read the text.*
- *Then do task 1.*
- *Write the answers to the questions in the table. Do not write sentences but write words or notes only. There is one example (0) at the beginning.*

	Questions	Answers
0	**In which town is Shrovetide Football played?**	**Ashbourne**
1	What is the filling of the ball?	
2	Sometimes a match ends before 10 pm on the first day. What is the reason?	
3	What is the name of the team from the north?	
4	How long is the distance between the goals?	
5	What are the players not allowed to do with the ball? Name one thing.	
6	From where exactly can you score a goal?	
7	What is the goal made of?	

Task 2

- *Read the text again.*
- *Then read the headlines.*
- *Choose the correct headline for each paragraph (A–G) of the text.*
- *Write the letter of the paragraph in the box next to the headline. There is one more headline than you need. There is an example (0) at the beginning.*

	Headlines	Paragraphs
0	**Shrovetide Football is a very traditional game.**	**A**
1	Why a player plays on one side or the other	
2	The playing time	
3	The players east of Ashbourne	
4	The rules of the game	
5	How a scorer is celebrated	
6	The tasks of the different players	
7	What the ball looks like	

Zweiter Prüfungsteil: Wortschatz – Schreiben

Aufgabe 4: Wortschatz

4.1 Free time – Part 1

- Complete the following text (sentences 1–6) with words from the box.
- Use each word only <u>once</u>.
- There is <u>one more word</u> than you need.

on	times	really	about	already	perhaps	every

Tracy and Ranjeev are talking about their free time:

Tracy: I'm absolutely mad _____ (1) football. I go to football practice three _____ (2) a week. And I play in a match almost _____ (3) weekend.

Ranjeev: I play the guitar in a band. We've _____ (4) played some concerts in our youth club. We are _____ (5) good. _____ (6) we'll take part in a TV casting show this summer.

4.2 At Kenton School – Part 2

Complete the following text (sentences 1–6) with <u>suitable</u> words.

Peter, a student from Germany, is talking about his experience at Kenton School in Great Britain.

1. I _____ the last six months at Kenton School in Newcastle.
2. It's a great school so I had a good _____ there.
3. The _____ in my tutor group were very friendly.
4. Lessons started at 9 am, which means I didn't have to get up as _____ as in Germany.
5. Like everybody else I had to _____ school uniform: black shoes, dark trousers, shirt and tie. I looked great ☺!
6. Most lessons were _____, but I found History and Science quite boring.

Aufgabe 5: Schreiben

Moving to Germany

Imagine:
Martin *(15) is a student <u>at your school</u>. He spent the last summer holidays at a campsite in Spain with his parents. There they made friends with their Spanish neighbours: Juan (15) and his father. Sadly, Juan's father had just lost his job as a technician at a big Spanish company.*

After the holidays, Martin got an email from Juan – in English, of course, because Martin speaks no Spanish and Juan no German.

- Read Juan's email and write back to him.
- Answer <u>all</u> his questions.
- Think of a nice <u>beginning</u> and a nice <u>ending</u> to your email.
- Write <u>100 words</u> or more.
- Write an email with <u>complete sentences</u>.

Hi Martin,

Great news! My dad has got a new job! And guess where?! In the company where your dad works! My dad can start his job on 1st September! We both hope that learning German won't be too difficult.

We'll move to Germany next month. So we'll soon be able to do lots of things together. **What can young people do in your town in their free time?**

I'll go to the same school as you do, I think. **What is a typical school day like?** (I hope the food in your school canteen is not too healthy ☺. I love pizza and hamburgers for lunch.)

I also hope school is not too stressful in Germany – so **what about homework and tests or exams**?

I'd really like to get some work experience before I leave school. **How does your school help with that?**

Soon I'll be able to talk to you in German – that'll be great.

Tchuss! (You taught me that word in the summer. I hope the spelling is OK.)

Juan

Lösungsvorschläge

Erster Prüfungsteil: Hörverstehen – Leseverstehen

Hauptschulabschluss Haupttermin

Wichtige Hinweise:
Alle Texte, die im Folgenden zu hören sind, werden zweimal vorgespielt. Vor dem ersten Hören wird Zeit gegeben, sich mit den Aufgaben vertraut zu machen. Der Hörverstehenstest besteht aus zwei Teilen:

Aufgabe 1: Hörverstehen Teil 1: *The Tube*

The London Underground plays a big part in the lives of Londoners. In 2013 the London Underground celebrated its 150th birthday. Listen to Jackie and Richard from Urban News.
First read the tasks (1–6). Then listen to the programme. Tick the correct box or complete the sentences while you are listening. Tick only <u>one</u> box. At the end you will hear the programme again. Now read the tasks (1–6). You have <u>1 minute</u> to do this.
Now listen to the programme and do the tasks.

1 JACKIE: Hello, this is Jackie and …
   RICHARD: Richard from Urban News with "Special Sights in Britain". The London Underground is our topic today. Why? Well, it's 150 years old and – love it or hate it – the Underground is used by millions of Londoners and
5 tourists every day. So Jackie and I would like to tell you the story of how it all began.
   JACKIE: The Metro. The Subway. Whatever you call it, for Londoners, it's the Tube. – Well, 150 years – that's not bad for an underground, is it?
   RICHARD: Yes, it's amazing. The first part of the London Underground started in
10 1863. It was the Metropolitan line which opened between Paddington and Farringdon on the 10th January. The Metropolitan line was the world's first underground railway.
   JACKIE: In 1863 – when building the underground began – digging huge tunnels under London meant digging them by hand. So, using only hand tools and
15 having no machines – wow, that must have been really hard work!
   RICHARD: Oh yeah! – And when they started the underground in 1863 they used steam trains, right?
   [Jackie: Yep.]

They had steam trains and carriages made of wood. And the steam trains used real coal fires pushing steam into the air! Steam filled the tunnels and caused breathing difficulties. The sight and smell of steam and smoke was everywhere. And I think they only said goodbye to the last steam train in 1961. It's unbelievable.

JACKIE: That's right. – But the Tube has been more than just a transport system, especially during the Second World War – when London was being bombed. During that time people actually slept in the tunnels overnight and there were even beds in there.

RICHARD: Very true. – And do you also remember the days when smoking was allowed on the underground?

JACKIE: Oh yes.

RICHARD: I'm a non-smoker, so you can imagine that I didn't really like it. I mean today it's amazing to think that you could smoke on the underground.

JACKIE: But then smoking was banned after a fire at King's Cross Station in 1987. People couldn't use the station for some time though it is one of the busiest stations on the Tube network. And ... well, you know, it has always been especially popular with tourists.

Thinking of all these tourists coming to London and travelling on the tube we do have some advice for them, don't we, Richard.

RICHARD: Yes! First thing of course, you need a map. – Now the London Underground map is fantastically designed. It's easy to read. But it's different from reality, so don't mix it up with a street map.

JACKIE: Right. – But perhaps the most important and the most famous advice for tourists is …

RICHARD: Mind the gap.

JACKIE: Hahaha … Exactly. But do you know why? Well, the old tunnels followed the streets above. The streets are not straight, they are curved. That's why there is a gap between the trains and the platforms.

RICHARD: So be careful! Mind the warning!

JACKIE/Richard: Mind the gap! – Hahaha.

> Now listen to the programme again and check your answers.

1. c

    Hinweis: "It was the Metropolitan line which opened between Paddington and Farringdon on the 10th January." (Z. 10f.)

2. Workers had to dig tunnels under the city **by hand**.

    Hinweis: "In 1863 – when building the underground began – digging huge Tunnels under London meant digging them by hand." (Z. 13f.)

3. b
   Hinweis: "Steam filled the tunnels and caused breathing difficulties." (Z. 20f.)

4. When the city was being bombed in the Second World War Londoners **slept** in the tunnels.
   Hinweis: "During that time people actually slept in the tunnels overnight ..." (Z. 26)

5. c
   Hinweis: "People couldn't use the station for some time though ..." (Z. 34)

6. a
   Hinweis: "So be careful! Mind the warning!" (Z. 48)

Aufgabe 2: Hörverstehen Teil 2: *McDonald's*

> *You are going to hear a radio program called 'Success Stories in the USA'. Lynn McCain and Anthony Johnson are talking about the history of McDonald's restaurants.*
> *First read the tasks (1–6). Then listen to the program. Tick the correct box or complete the sentences while you are listening. Tick only <u>one</u> box. At the end you will hear the program again. Now read the tasks (1–6). You have <u>1 minute</u> to do this.*
> *Now listen to the program and do the tasks.*

JOSH: Hello to everybody and welcome to "Success stories in the USA". One of the first letters a child learns these days is "M"– not for Mummy or Mama, but for – McDonald's. The golden "M" is one of the best-known logos in the world and McDonald's one of America's biggest successes in the food industry. – Lynn McCaine and Anthony Johnson have the story behind the name.

ANTHONY: The McDonald's story began almost 75 years ago: on May 15, 1940, two brothers, Richard and Maurice McDonald, opened a restaurant in San Bernadino, California. It was a typical American drive-in restaurant with waiters and waitresses and a long menu.

LYNN: In 1948, the McDonald brothers made some important changes: they had no waiters or waitresses anymore and the menu was a lot shorter. The food was so easy to make that trained cooks were no longer needed. So the restaurant was a lot cheaper to run.

ANTHONY: The McDonald brothers' concept was a big success and they opened other restaurants in the same style – but only in and around California. That changed one day in 1954, when Ray Kroc visited the San Bernadino restaurant. Kroc was absolutely fascinated by the McDonalds' concept, made a deal with the brothers, bought the licence and opened restaurants all over the US, all with the same menu and the same design.

LYNN: A few years later, the company went global, opening restaurants in Canada and Puerto Rico. In 1971 they crossed the Atlantic to open the first McDonald's in Europe. And it was not London as everybody would think. They first went to Zaandam, a little Dutch town near Amsterdam. Munich in Germany followed a few months later. The first British McDonald's opened in London only three years after that.

ANTHONY: Well, today London has got 72 McDonald's, and worldwide there are now more than 34,000. McDonald's serves about 70 million people each day and employs around 2 million people. Whatever you think of McDonald's, it's just one of the greatest marketing ideas the world has ever seen.

LYNN: By the way, have you ever wondered where the name *Hamburger* comes from? The name comes from the town of Hamburg.

ANTHONY: Hamburg? In Germany?

LYNN: Yes! Here's the story: in the 19th century a huge number of European immigrants travelled from Hamburg to New York by ship. At the time, meatballs – called *Frikadellen* in German – were very popular in and around Hamburg. And soon restaurants in New York offered those meatballs, too, and called them Hamburg Steaks. And then, around the year 1900, someone had the idea to sell Hamburg Steaks between two pieces of bread, like sandwiches, and people simply called them Hamburgers.

ANTHONY: How interesting!

JOSH: Haha … Next week, Lynn and Anthony are going to talk about …

> Now listen to the program again and check your answers.

1. McDonald's will soon celebrate its **75**th birthday.
   Hinweis: "The McDonald's story began almost 75 years ago: on May 15, 1940 …" (Z. 7)

2. c
   Hinweis: "In 1948, the McDonald brothers made some important changes: they had no waiters or waitresses anymore …" (Z. 11f.)

3. a
   Hinweis: "That changed one day in 1954, when Ray Kroc visited the San Bernadino restaurant. Kroc was absolutely fascinated by the McDonald's concept, made a deal with the brothers, bought the licence …" (Z. 16ff.)

4. c
   ✒ *Hinweis:* "They first went to Zaandam, a little Dutch town near Amsterdam." (Z. 24)

5. Worldwide, around **2/two** million people work for McDonald's.
   ✒ *Hinweis:* "McDonald's serves about 70 million people each day and employs around 2 million people." (Z. 28f.)

6. Restaurants in New York called the meat in the burgers **Hamburg Steaks**.
   ✒ *Hinweis:* "And soon restaurants in New York offered those meatballs, too, and called them Hamburg Steaks." (Z. 37f.)

Ende des Hörverstehenstests.

Aufgabe 3: Leseverstehen

Task 1:

1. cork
   ✒ *Hinweis:* "Strangely enough the ball is filled with cork …" (Z. 12f.)

2. a goal after 5 pm
   ✒ *Hinweis:* "If a player scores a goal after 5 pm, the match ends on that day …" (Z. 26ff.)

3. Up'ards
   ✒ *Hinweis:* "The players who were born north of Henmore River are the Up'ards." (Z. 36ff.)

4. 3 miles
   ✒ *Hinweis:* "They must take the ball to a small stone wall near the river west of the town – three miles away from the stone wall in the east." (Z. 42ff.)

5. hide the ball / transport the ball in a motor vehicle / …
   ✒ *Hinweis:* "But it must not be hidden or transported in a motor vehicle and …" (Z. 55f.)

6. the river / …
   ✒ *Hinweis:* "And – the player who wants to score a goal has to stand in Henmore River …" (Z. 63ff.)

7. stone

   Hinweis: "and throw the ball three times against the small stone wall which serves as the goal." (Z. 65ff.)

Task 2:
1. D

   Hinweis: "Well, Henmore River flows through the town and splits the city into two parts – and two teams." (Z. 33ff.)

2. C

   Hinweis: "It starts at 2 pm and has to finish by 10 pm on each day." (Z. 22f.)

3. –

4. E

   Hinweis: "As there is no referee you could think that the game ends in fights. But this is not the case because there are things the players have to accept: ..." (Z. 48ff.)

5. G

   Hinweis: "When a player has scored a goal he is carried back into the town on the team-players' shoulders and cheered by hundreds of tourists. And he gets the hand-painted ball as a prize." (Z. 71ff.)

6. F

   Hinweis: "Some of the players train to be runners; others train as 'river specialists'" (Z. 60f.)

7. B

   Hinweis: "Strangely enough the ball is filled with cork and it is bigger and heavier than a standard football. What makes the ball unique is that it is hand-painted ..." (Z. 12ff.)

Zweiter Prüfungsteil: Wortschatz – Schreiben

Aufgabe 4: Wortschatz

4.1 Free time – Part 1

1. Tracy: I'm absolutely mad **about** football.

2. I go to football practice three **times** a week.

3. And I play in a match almost **every** weekend.

4. Ranjeev: I play the guitar in a band. We've **already** played some concerts in our youth club.
5. We are **really** good.
6. **Perhaps** we'll take part in a TV casting show this summer.

4.2 At Kenton School – Part 2

1. I **spent** the last six months at Kenton School in Newcastle.
2. It's a great school so I had a good **time** there.
3. The **pupils/students/people** in my tutor group were very friendly.
4. Lessons started at 9 am, which means I didn't have to get up as **early** as in Germany.
5. Like everybody else I had to **wear** school uniform: black shoes, dark trousers, shirt and tie. I looked great ☺!
6. Most lessons were **interesting/exciting/fun**, but I found History and Science quite boring.

Aufgabe 5: Schreiben

Hinweis: Lies dir die Aufgabenstellung und die E-Mail von Juan genau durch, bevor du anfängst zu schreiben. Beachte dabei Folgendes:
1. Beantworte <u>alle</u> Fragen, die Juan in seiner Mail stellt.
2. Finde einen passenden Anfang (Begrüßung) und ein passendes Ende (Verabschiedung) für Martins E-Mail.
3. Schreibe <u>100 Wörter</u> oder mehr.
4. Schreibe Martins Antwort in ganzen Sätzen.

Hi Juan,

What a surprise! Your dad has a new job in my dad's company? I can't believe it. It's great news! We'll be together every day, because we'll go to the same school, and we'll be able to do a lot of things together.
I play for a junior football team in our town. I know you are a good player, so join our team and we'll score lots of goals!
And there is a big shopping centre in our town. We can have burgers and ice cream there and hang out with my friends. It's the meeting point for young people in our town.
You asked me about our school. School is from 8 am to 4 pm from Monday to Thursday. Friday we finish at 2 pm. There are two breaks, one in the morning

and one at lunch time. You are lucky, our school canteen sometimes offers pizza and hamburgers for lunch.

School is not stressful, but there is homework and we write a lot of tests. There are final exams in Maths, German and English at the end of Year 10. Some teachers are stricter than others. But I think you'll do well.

You asked me about work experience before you leave school. Once a week someone from the job centre in our town helps each of us to find work experience. He gives advice on how to plan our future. He is very nice and I'm sure that he'll help you, too.

Tschüss, and don't forget the dots next time ;-)

Take care,

Martin   *(267 words)*

> **Zentrale Prüfung am Ende der Klasse 10 – NRW –
> Hauptschule Typ A / Gesamtschule GK – Englisch 2015**

Erster Prüfungsteil: Hörverstehen – Leseverstehen

Aufgabe 1: Hörverstehen Teil 1

The Brit School

You are going to hear a radio programme from the "Brit School's" own radio station. Laura Ashton and Jamie Stuart talk about their school – the Brit School.

- *First read the tasks.*
- *Then listen to the interview.*
- *While you are listening, tick the correct box or complete the sentences.*
- *At the end you will hear the interview again.*
- *Now read the tasks. You have <u>1 minute</u> to do this.*

Now listen to the interview and do the tasks.

1. The *Brit School* ...
   a) ☐ creates stars.
   b) ☐ is near London.
   c) ☐ teaches languages.

2. The headmaster says the *Brit* ...
   a) ☐ is a private school.
   b) ☐ is for rich students only.
   c) ☐ doesn't cost students any money.

3. The *Brit* offers the students all they need to become a _____ in show business.

4. *Brit* students like their school so much because ...
   a) ☐ everyone there loves art.
   b) ☐ the building is absolutely great.
   c) ☐ there are no normal school subjects.

5. The *Brit School* ...
   a) ☐ cares little about good grades.
   b) ☐ only takes on a limited number of students.
   c) ☐ expects their students to study on Saturdays.

6. If you don't want to be a star you can find a job as a stage manager or _____.

Aufgabe 2: Hörverstehen Teil 2

Inuvik Sunrise Festival

You are going to hear a radio program with Jeremy and Michael who are talking about the Inuvik Sunrise Festival, a very special three-day event in the Arctic areas of Canada.

- *First read the tasks.*
- *Then listen to the interview.*
- *While you are listening, tick the correct box or complete the sentences.*
- *At the end you will hear the interview again.*
- *Now read the tasks. You have 1 minute to do this.*

Now listen to the interview and do the tasks.

1. Inuvik is …
   a) ☐ a country.
   b) ☐ a big event.
   c) ☐ a small place.

2. In the Arctic there is no sun from December to _____.

3. People on the ice-field were excited because of the first _____.

4. One of the attractions was …
   a) ☐ a snowmobile race.
   b) ☐ an ice shaping contest.
   c) ☐ an animal competition.

5. Jason Nasogaluak says nowadays the Inuit people travel with _____.

6. In May …
   a) ☐ there is a big festival.
   b) ☐ hunting is not allowed.
   c) ☐ the sun shines all day long.

Aufgabe 3: Leseverstehen

My first step to becoming president
by Chris van Allsburg

When I was about nine years old, my father bought me a go-kart. It was fire-engine-red and had a beautiful motor on the back. It was a dream come true. But I had to promise to my father that I would never, never use the kart if he wasn't around. If I did, no more go-kart.

At that time our driveway[1] was just dirt[2]. But one morning an asphalt truck pulled up to our house, and by the afternoon we had a beautiful smooth asphalt driveway, the only one in the neighborhood.

A few days later my mom and dad had to go out for the afternoon. After they had left, my friend Steve came over. We didn't know what to do and so we went to look at my go-kart in the garage. Pretty soon we were rolling the kart out on the drive. I thought, "One little ride won't hurt. Besides, Dad will never know."

I checked the tank. Empty. We kept extra petrol in a big canister. Steve and I carried the full canister across the driveway and lifted it up. Unfortunately, it was too heavy for us. We got one gallon into the kart and about nine gallons onto the driveway.

Do you know what happens to fresh asphalt when petrol gets on it? It just melts[3] away. Steve and I stared at the hole in our driveway.

I rolled the kart back into the garage. I knew I was in big trouble because I had broken my promise about not using the go-kart. I felt so bad. I waited for my parents to come home, feeling worse every minute. Finally, they arrived and parked right over the hole. They hadn't noticed it. Wasn't I lucky! But I knew, sooner or later, they would see it and ask questions. What should I tell them? I thought, "I'll just blame[4] it on the car. Everybody knows tanks can leak and lose petrol, right?"

My mom made dinner, but I didn't have much of an appetite. I just couldn't wait till they saw the hole and the idea of telling a lie made me sick. It was too much for me. Before we had dessert, I asked my dad to come out on the driveway with me and I told him everything. I think I was even crying a little bit. My dad moved the car and looked at the hole. I expected the worst. "Well ...," he said, "that's not too bad ... Let's go back and have some ice cream."

My dad took the kart away, but only for a few weeks. When I went to my room that night I felt pretty lucky. Lying in bed, I remembered a story about how young George Washington[5] cut down an apple tree. When his father discovered the fallen tree, George said, "I did it with my little axe, father." George didn't get into real trouble because he had told the truth. "Wow," I thought, "I just did that myself!" I fell asleep thinking, "Maybe one day I'll be president, too!"

---

1 driveway – way to the house
2 dirt – here: *unbefestigter Schotterweg*
3 melt – ice melts in the sun because it is too warm
4 to blame someone – *jemandem die Schuld für etwas geben*
5 George Washington – first American President

My first step to becoming president

- *First read the text.*
- *Then do the tasks 1–11.*
- *For tasks 1, 2, 3, 6 and 10 tick the correct box.*
- *For tasks 4, 5, 7, 8 and 9 fill in the information.*
- *For task 11 write down your answer. You need not write complete sentences.*

1. The father gave his little boy a ...
   a) ☐ fire-engine.
   b) ☐ go-kart.
   c) ☐ promise.

2. When the storyteller was a child his family ...
   a) ☐ had a truck.
   b) ☐ got a new driveway.
   c) ☐ moved to a new neighborhood.

3. When his parents went out one day the storyteller and his friend ...
   a) ☐ were bored.
   b) ☐ rolled the kart onto the street.
   c) ☐ went for a ride on the go-kart.

4. The two boys had problems with the petrol canister because it
   _____.

5. When the two boys were filling the petrol in the tank two things happened:
   a) _____
   b) _____

6. The storyteller was afraid because ...
   a) ☐ he hadn't kept his promise.
   b) ☐ his parents were not at home.
   c) ☐ he couldn't put the car back into the garage.

7. After his father had parked the car in the driveway the boy felt a bit better. Why?
   _____.

8. The storyteller first thought of giving the following excuse:
   _____.

9. At dinnertime the storyteller didn't feel well. Find two examples in the text.
   a) _____
   b) _____

10. The storyteller ...
   a) ☐ could never ride his kart again.
   b) ☐ didn't get any dessert that evening.
   c) ☐ didn't expect this father's reaction.

11. Why did the storyteller's father react the way he did? Give a reason.
   _____.

Zweiter Prüfungsteil: Wortschatz – Schreiben

Aufgabe 4: Wortschatz

4.1 Jobs in Britain – Part 1

- *Complete the following text (sentences 1–6) with words from the box.*
- *Use each word only <u>once</u>.*
- *There is <u>one more word</u> than you need.*

| experience | worry | different | advantage | difficult | offer | exercise |

The following text is about working in Britain.

1. You speak English. So why not get some work _____ in Britain?

2. Don't _____, your English doesn't have to be perfect.

3. It is not _____ to get information about jobs in Britain on the Internet.

4. In the summer holidays places like cafés, restaurants or hotels, for example, often _____ summer jobs.

5. A job in Britain means you get to know a _____ way of life.

6. Another _____ is that your English gets better.

4.2 Part 2

Complete the following text (sentences 1–6) with <u>suitable</u> words.

The following text gives you some tips for job interviews.

1. It is important to _____ the right clothes.
2. You should _____ a few minutes early.
3. Do not _____ questions with "Yes" or "No" only.
4. Don't use slang! Always use polite _____.
5. Make clear why you are _____ in getting the job.
6. If you follow these tips, you will have a better _____ of getting the job.

Aufgabe 5: Schreiben

You are planning to get a summer job somewhere in Britain after leaving school. On the Internet you have found the following job advertisements.

- Read the job advertisements.
- Choose one job you want to apply for.

 We need you!!!!

Our café in London is looking for young people who would like to join our service team.

You should …
- be 16 or older
- have some work experience in restaurants or coffee shops
- be flexible about working times and weekend shifts
- enjoy working in a team
- be friendly and make customers feel welcome

You get …
- the chance to be part of a great new team
- training on the job
- fair pay

If you are interested, contact: kamps@london.com

Illustrationen Backwaren © Can Stock Photo Inc./yupiramos

or

Join our team!

Edinburgh Central Youth Hostel is looking for a **hostel assistant**.
- August – September 2015
- 20 hours per week (morning or afternoons)
- room and meals included

We need you …
- on the reception desk (check in/check out)
- for housekeeping (making beds/cleaning)

If you want to apply you should …
- be at least 16
- speak more than one language
- like to work in a team
- be able to work under pressure
- be friendly

Send your application to:
applications@syhoa.org.uk

Flagge © Maxx-Studio. Shutterstock; Karte © Can Stock Photo Inc./bogdanserban

---

Write your <u>*email application*</u> *for* <u>*the job you choose*</u>.
Include the following information:
- *personal details*
- *general interests*
- *motivation specially for this job*
- *qualifications*

Write about <u>*120 words*</u>. *Remember the formals aspects.*

Lösungsvorschläge

Erster Prüfungsteil: Hörverstehen – Leseverstehen

> *Hauptschulabschluss Haupttermin*
>
> *Wichtige Hinweise:*
> *Alle Texte, die im Folgenden zu hören sind, werden zweimal vorgespielt. Vor dem ersten Hören wird Zeit gegeben, sich mit den Aufgaben vertraut zu machen.*
> *Der Hörverstehenstest besteht aus zwei Teilen:*

Aufgabe 1: Hörverstehen Teil 1: *The Brit School*

> *You are going to hear a radio programme from the "Brit School's" own radio station. Laura Ashton and Jamie Stuart talk about their school – the Brit School. First read the tasks. Then listen to the interview. While you are listening, tick the correct box or complete the sentences. At the end you will hear the interview again. Now read the tasks. You have 1 minute to do this.*
> *Now listen to the interview and do the tasks.*

1   LAURA ASHTON: Hello everybody, this is "Brit FM", the Brit School's own radio station. You're listening to Laura Ashton and Jamie Stuart. We're here with today's special: our School – the Brit School.
   JAMIE STUART: So you want to become a famous singer, an actor or an actress
5   like our famous graduates Amy Winehouse and Katie Melua? Then the Brit School is just right for you. The Brit – as we call it – is a school for Performing Arts and Technology in South London. Well, so what? There are other schools like this. But the Brit is not like the others, it's different. Listen to what our headmaster Stuart Worden says.
10   HEADMASTER: Well, most of Britain's performing arts schools are private schools for rich students because they are so expensive. The Brit School, however, is a state school, which means that going to this school is totally free. The Brit is mainly supported by the British Record Industry but it also gets support from friends in other arts industries.
15   LAURA ASHTON: Another way our school gets money is this: we put our own musicals, plays and concerts onto the stage. These shows earn well over £ 200,000 each year. And now – what can you learn at the Brit? Jamie.
   JAMIE STUART: A lot! You can learn everything you need to become a professional in show business. There are lots of classes like drama, dancing and re-

cording and also a number of workshops where you learn how to make costumes and equipment for the stage.

LAURA ASHTON: But what makes the Brit so special? – Well, what's absolutely great is that you meet people with the same interest as you – the arts. When you walk through the corridors of our school you'll find hundreds of teenagers trying out scenes from a drama or doing dance routines and having fun.

JAMIE STUART: Right. – But although the Brit is a school for the performing arts we have to do all the normal school subjects as well – such as maths, biology and history. But how can you get in?

LAURA ASHTON: Well – getting into the Brit is not that easy. Although the school offers 880 places there are more than 3,000 teenagers who want to get in every year. So it's not enough just to be good at school work. Brit students have to be creative, relaxed, confident – and willing to do lots of extra work, but not at the weekends. They're free!

JAMIE STUART: It takes a lot of time and energy to make the most of your talents. But there are excellent chances for your future even if you don't want to become a star. Many of us are interested in jobs behind the scenes as stage managers, sound engineers or set designers – we all know that these are just as important as the performance itself. So, try it and become the next Brit School student.

LAURA ASHTON: And that's it for today's topic "The Brit School". Next week we're going to present our famous ex-student …

> Now listen to the interview again and check your answers.

1. a

    Hinweis: "So you want to become a famous singer, an actor or an actress like our famous graduates Amy Winehouse and Katie Melua? Then the Brit School is just right for you." (Z. 4 ff.)

2. c

    Hinweis: "The Brit School, however, is a state school, which means that going to this school is totally free." (Z. 11 ff.)

3. The Brit offers the students all they need to become a **professional/star** in show business.

    Hinweis: "You can learn everything you need to become a professional in show business." (Z. 18 f.)

4. a

    Hinweis: "Well, what's absolutely great is that you meet people with the same interest as you – the arts." (Z. 22 f.)

5. b
   ✒ **Hinweis:** *"Although the school offers 880 places there are more than 3,000 teenagers who want to get in every year." (Z. 30 ff.)*
6. If you don't want to be a star you can find a job as a stage manager or **sound engineer/set designer**.
   ✒ **Hinweis:** *"But there are excellent chances for your future even if you don't want to become a star. Many of us are interested in jobs behind the scenes as stage managers, sound engineers or set designers ..." (Z. 36 ff.)*

Aufgabe 2: Hörverstehen Teil 2: *Inuvik Sunrise Festival*

> You are going to hear a radio program with Jeremy and Michael who are talking about the Inuvik Sunrise Festival, a very special three-day event in the Arctic areas of Canada.
> First read the tasks. Then listen to the interview. While you are listening, tick the correct box or complete the sentences. At the end you will hear the interview again. Now read the tasks. You have <u>1 minute</u> to do this.
> Now listen to the interview and do the tasks.

1 JEREMY: Hi everybody and welcome to our weekly radio show "Experience Canada". With me today is Michael Galore and our topic today is a great event we went to in the far northwest of our country, in a place called Inuvik – a small village 200 km north of the Arctic Circle.
5 MICHAEL: An amazing experience indeed! We were at this year's Inuvik Sunrise Festival, a three-day festival in the second week of January!
   JEREMY: But, Michael ... we first need to explain what this festival is about.
   MICHAEL: Oh yes (laughing) ... Sorry ... I forgot that our listeners might not know the famous Noon-Moon of the Arctic ...
10 JEREMY: Very famous!
   MICHAEL: Well ... in the mid-Arctic area, in the first week of December the sun sets for the last time below the horizon, and it won't rise again before the second week of January.
   JEREMY: Wow ... that's 30 days of darkness!
15 MICHAEL: True ... and this special sunrise is definitely a reason to celebrate, isn't it?
   JEREMY: It is! We stood outside the village centre ... on this ice-field with the 3,400 inhabitants of Inuvik and lots of tourists, and waited for the first sunshine.
20 MICHAEL: It was such an exciting atmosphere!

JEREMY: It definitely was! When the sun finally appeared, everybody cheered and shouted "Hooray!" – Even though this first daylight lasted just 45 MINUTES! – But ... Michael, what did you like best at the festival?

MICHAEL: Mmh, definitely the ice sculpture competition – people made wonderful animals out of ice, like eagles and whales! – And you, Jeremy?

JEREMY: Erm ... well ... I liked the snowmobile parade very much. But – my favorite attraction was the brand new Ice Road Café on the frozen lake. It was made out of snow, a gigantic igloo!

MICHAEL: Yeah, I liked it too – and ... you know, even Inuvik citizens were fascinated. I mean, igloos are common to the Arctic ... aren't they?

JEREMY: No, Michael, they aren't any longer! Jason Nasogaluak, who built the café, said that of course, nowadays, even the Inuit, the natives of the Arctic, don't live in igloos anymore but travel with modern tents.

MICHAEL: Oh ... talking about living in the Arctic – it must be really hard to do everything with a flashlight for about 6–8 weeks!

JEREMY: Oh yes! I wouldn't like it! But – from May onwards, they will have 24 hours of daylight again. I talked to Akiak, one of the Inuvik citizens, and he told me that he's looking forward to the extra hunting hours daylight brings.

MICHAEL: Oh yeah, that must be great for him. So everybody out there ... you see: Inuvik Sunlight Festival is worth a visit – be sure of that! Well ... thanks for listening today and tune in again next week for "Experience Canada"!

> Now listen to the interview again and check your answers.

1. c

   Hinweis: "... and our topic today is a great event we went to in the far northwest of our country, in a place called Inuvik – a small village 200 km north of the Arctic Circle." (Z. 2 ff.)

2. In the Arctic there is no sun from December to **January**.

   Hinweis: "Well ... in the mid-Arctic area, in the first week of December the sun sets for the last time below the horizon, and it won't rise again before the second week of January." (Z. 11 ff.)

3. People on the ice-field were excited because of the first **sunrise / sunshine / daylight**.

   Hinweis: "When the sun finally appeared, everybody cheered and shouted 'Hooray!' " (Z. 21 ff.)

4. b
   Hinweis: "Mmh, definitely the ice sculpture competition – people made wonderful animals out of ice, like eagles and whales!" (Z. 24 f.)

5. Jason Nasogaluak says nowadays the Inuit people travel with **(modern) tents**.
   Hinweis: "Jason Nasogaluak, who built the café, said that of course, nowadays, even the Inuit, the natives of the Arctic, don't live in igloos anymore but travel with modern tents." (Z. 31 ff.)

6. c
   Hinweis: "But – from May onwards, they will have 24 hours of daylight again." (Z. 36 f.)

Ende des Hörverstehenstests.

Aufgabe 3: Leseverstehen

1. b
   Hinweis: "When I was about nine years old, my father bought me a go-kart." (Z. 3 f.)

2. b
   Hinweis: "But one morning an asphalt truck pulled up to our house, and by the afternoon we had a beautiful smooth asphalt driveway, ..." (Z. 12 ff.)

3. a
   Hinweis: "We didn't know what to do and so we went to look at my go-kart in the garage." (Z. 20 ff.)

4. The two boys had problems with the petrol canister because it **was too heavy**.
   Hinweis: "Unfortunately, it was too heavy for us." (Z. 29 f.)

5. a) Petrol got on the driveway./The asphalt melted away.
   b) Now there was a hole.
   Hinweis: "Do you know what happens to fresh asphalt when petrol gets on it? It just melts away. Steve and I stared at the hole in our driveway." (Z. 33 ff.)

6. a
   Hinweis: "I knew I was in big trouble because I had broken my promise about not using the go-kart." (Z. 37 ff.)

7. His parents had parked their car over the hole./
They hadn't noticed/seen the hole.
Hinweis: "Finally, they arrived and parked right over the hole. They hadn't noticed it. Wasn't I lucky!" (Z. 42 ff.)

8. The car loses petrol./The car has a leak.
Hinweis: " 'I'll just blame it on the car. Everybody knows tanks can leak and lose petrol, right?' " (Z. 47 ff.)

9. a) I didn't have much of an appetite/… the idea of telling a lie made me sick.
Hinweis: "My mom made dinner, but I didn't have much of an appetite. I just couldn't wait till they saw the hole and the idea of telling a lie made me sick." (Z. 50 ff.)
   b) I think I was even crying a little bit.
Hinweis: "I think I was even crying a little bit." (Z. 57)

10. c
Hinweis: "When I went to my room that night I felt pretty lucky." (Z. 63 f.)

11. His son (had) told him the truth./He didn't tell a lie./His dad thought what his son had done was not too bad/not a big deal.
Hinweis: "Lying in bed, I remembered a story about how young George Washington cut down an apple tree. When his father discovered the fallen tree, George said, 'I did it with my little axe, father.' George didn't get into real trouble because he had told the truth. 'Wow,' I thought, 'I just did that myself!' " (Z. 65 ff.)

Zweiter Prüfungsteil: Wortschatz – Schreiben

Aufgabe 4: Wortschatz

4.1 Jobs in Britain – Part 1

1. You speak English. So why not get some work **experience** in Britain?
2. Don't **worry**, your English doesn't have to be perfect.
3. It is not **difficult** to get information about jobs in Britain on the Internet.
4. In the summer holidays places like cafés, restaurants or hotels, for example, often **offer** summer jobs.
5. A job in Britain means you get to know a **different** way of life.
6. Another **advantage** is that your English gets better.

4.2 Part 2

1. It is important to **wear / put on / choose** the right clothes.
2. You should **be there / arrive** a few minutes early.
3. Do not **answer / react** to questions with "Yes" or "No" only.
4. Don't use slang! Always use polite **language / words**.
5. Make clear why you are **interested** in getting the job.
6. If you follow these tips, you will have a better **chance** of getting the job.

Aufgabe 5: Schreiben

Hinweis: Lies dir die Aufgabenstellung und die Anzeigen genau durch, bevor du anfängst zu schreiben. Entscheide dich für <u>eine</u> der beiden Anzeigen. Beachte beim Schreiben deiner E-Mail folgende Punkte:

1. Schreibe etwas zu allen vier genannten Punkten:
   personal details *(Angaben zu deiner Person)*,
   general interests *(allgemeine Interessen)*,
   motivation specially for this job *(Gründe, wieso du gerade an diesem Job interessiert bist)*,
   qualifications *(Kenntnisse/Fähigkeiten, die dich für diesen Job geeignet machen)*
2. Finde einen passenden Anfang (Begrüßungsformel) und ein passendes Ende (Schlussformel). Schreibe in einem höflichen Stil und verwende keine Umgangssprache!

3. Schreibe auf jeden Fall mehr als 120 Wörter.
4. Schreibe deine E-Mail in ganzen Sätzen.

Beispiellösung Anzeige 1:

Dear Sir or Madam,

I'd like to apply for a job in the service team of your café in London. I am 17 years old and I finish school in June this year. English is one of my favourite subjects.

I think that I have a lot of qualities needed for this job. For example, I have some work experience in cafés in Cologne, doing a variety of tasks. Besides I am very flexible when it comes to working hours and I do not mind doing weekend shifts. Working in a team and making customers happy has always been important to me. Please find my CV attached.

In my free time, I play tennis in a club. Furthermore, I am a very sociable person and I find it easy to make friends. I would be pleased to be part of your team. Working with people and living in an exciting city like London at the same time has always been my dream.

I am looking forward to hearing from you.

Yours faithfully,

(Your name) *(173 words)*

Beispiellösung Anzeige 2:

Dear Sir or Madam,

I'm applying for the job of hostel assistant at your youth hostel in Edinburgh in August and September 2015.

I am 16 years old, and I graduate in June this year. I think I have the qualities needed for this job. I speak three languages, Turkish, German and English. Furthermore, I have been used to housekeeping, and looking after my younger brothers and sisters. I also like working with people. I would enjoy working at the reception desk. Besides, I am aware that teamwork is important in that job, and that you should always be friendly even if you have to work under pressure. Please find my CV attached.

In my free time I play football and travel a lot. I went to Spain last summer, for example. It would not be difficult for me to live in another country.

I am looking forward to hearing from you.

Yours faithfully,

(Your name) *(154 words)*

**Zentrale Prüfung am Ende der Klasse 10 – NRW –
Hauptschulabschluss – Englisch 2016**

Erster Prüfungsteil: Hörverstehen – Leseverstehen

Aufgabe 1: Hörverstehen Teil 1

The Thames Tunnel

You are going to hear an interview with Melinda Gordon and Thomas Carrey. They talk about something that once was called the 8th Wonder of the World: the Thames Tunnel.

- *First read the tasks.*
- *Then listen to the interview.*
- *While you are listening, tick the correct box or write down the information needed.*
- *At the end you will hear the interview again.*
- *Now read the tasks. You have 1 minute to do this.*

Now listen to the interview and do the tasks.

1. In the 19th century London needed a tunnel because there was …
   a) ☐ too much traffic.
   b) ☐ only a small harbour.
   c) ☐ just one bridge across the Thames.

2. Workers had to deal with some difficulties. Write down two.
   a) _____
   b) _____

3. When the tunnel opened …
   a) ☐ everything was finished.
   b) ☐ people could get through it on foot.
   c) ☐ horses could carry things from one side to the other.

4. There were attractions during a fair in the tunnel. Write down one.
   _____

5. From 1865 on, the tunnel has been used for:
   _____

Aufgabe 2: Hörverstehen Teil 2

How to join Canada's RCMP

Police officer Bill Fordy informs students at Surrey High School about how to start a career with the Royal Canadian Mounted Police, who are called Mounties. Student leader Alex Smith asks him some questions.

- *First read the tasks.*
- *Then listen to the interview.*
- *While you are listening, tick the correct box or write down the information needed.*
- *At the end you will hear the interview again.*
- *Now read the tasks. You have 1 minute to do this.*

Now listen to the interview and do the tasks.

1. Which basic characteristics should a Mountie have? Name <u>one</u>.
   _____

2. To apply for a job as a Mountie you must …
   a) ☐ be born in Canada.
   b) ☐ be a citizen of Canada.
   c) ☐ speak a bit of French.

3. To start working for the RCMP you must …
   a) ☐ be at least 18 years old.
   b) ☐ be able to drive special cars.
   c) ☐ have completed secondary school.

4. The RCMP sports program helps students to …
   a) ☐ get slim.
   b) ☐ build up their body.
   c) ☐ be ready for the job challenges.

5. It is most stressful for Mounties to …
   a) ☐ use their gun.
   b) ☐ chase criminals.
   c) ☐ help injured people.

6. RCMP applicants …
   a) ☐ choose where to work.
   b) ☐ work 24 hours a day.
   c) ☐ study before they start policing.

Aufgabe 3: Leseverstehen

Amanda and the wounded birds
by Colby Rodowsky

Being the daughter of Dr. Emma Hart wasn't always easy. Mom was running a "call-in show" on a radio, which means she talked to people on the phone who asked her help with their problems. Mom really cared about the people who phoned her. She was calling them her "wounded birds" – not during the show, of course, and never to anyone but me.
To me it sometimes felt like she spent much more time caring for her patients than caring for me, her daughter.
Mom was busier than she had ever been before and I wanted to see more of her. Besides that, I needed to talk to her. I had no major crisis, but there was Mr. Burnside, my English teacher, who asked me if I had thought about my career. I said I didn't even know where I wanted to go to college. "And what does your mother say?" he asked. I didn't tell him that she'd never found the time to talk with me about my career.
"Anybody else may call her and talk to her about important matters on the telephone," I thought, while I was walking home from school. I remembered her saying that she especially liked it when kids called her in the Dr. Emma Hart Show. And then – it crossed my mind: If anybody can call her, well, why can't I, her own daughter?
At home I practiced making my voice deeper than usual. Then I took a deep breath and I dialed the number of Mom's studio. I almost panicked when I heard the voice of Jordan, Mom's assistant, at the other end. I gave my name as Claire and told her that I wanted to talk to Dr. Hart because I needed her advice.
Then, all of a sudden I heard my mother's voice at the other end. Gosh, I mean, there I was, pretending to be Claire and talking to my own mother on the phone about my problems. I told her that I never got the chance to talk to my Mom because she was always too busy.
"Well Claire," Dr. Hart said. "To me the relationship between you and your mother doesn't seem too bad at all. I think she must know how you feel and therefore you need to tell her about your problems. So ask her for a proper date and tell her that you need more time with her. And, call me again to tell me if it worked out well."
When Mom got home that evening I knew it wasn't going to work. It had been a bad day for her, and she talked to me the whole evening about some problems of her wounded birds'.
On Friday I called Dr. Emma Hart again and told her that her suggestion hadn't worked. "Did you really try?" she asked. "Yes – eh – no, not really. She was very busy with her own problems and wouldn't listen to me", I said. And then, all of a sudden, the words were slipping out and I couldn't stop: "You know, the thing about my mother is that she has all these wounded birds who take all the time she has." Dead silence, it seemed to last forever, and I thought about running away from home, or at least hanging up.
When Mom finally spoke, her voice sounded shocked. She said: "I've been talking to Claire, who is really Amanda. From what I know of Amanda, she normally would have run away. But this time she didn't. She just hung on. Amanda is my daughter, and it seems we have some urgent things to talk about. What about spending the evening at our favorite restaurant, Amanda?"

"Amanda and the Wounded Birds" by Colby Rodowsky, copyright © 1987 by Colby Rodowsky; from VISIONS edited by Donald R. Gallo. Used by permission of Delacorte Press, an imprint of Random House Children's Books, a division of Penguin Random House LLC. All rights reserved.

Fill in the information needed or tick the correct box <u>and</u> support your answer by quoting from the text.

1. The narrator of the story is Dr. E. Hart's …

   _____

2. Dr. Emma Hart asks people for their opinion on the radio.
   This sentence is
   a) ☐ true   b) ☐ false
   because the text says

   _____

3. Dr. Hart addresses people on the phone as 'wounded birds'.
   This sentence is
   a) ☐ true   b) ☐ false
   because the text says

   _____

4. Amanda was having big trouble at school.
   This sentence is
   a) ☐ true   b) ☐ false
   because the text says

   _____

5. Amanda's main problem was …

   _____

6. On her way home, Amanda had an idea.
   This sentence is
   a) ☐ true   b) ☐ false
   because the text says

   _____

7. In the evening Amanda told her mother about what was troubling her.
   This sentence is
   a) ☐ true   b) ☐ false
   because the text says

   _____

8. Dr. Hart finally realized that she was talking to her daughter. How did she know?
   _____

Zweiter Prüfungsteil: Wortschatz – Schreiben

Aufgabe 4: Wortschatz

4.1 Work and Travel in Canada – Part 1

- *Complete the following text (sentences 1–6) with words from the box.*
- *Use each word only <u>once</u>.*
- *There is <u>one more word</u> than you need.*

get	important	job	see	culture	sponsor	work

1. I've just finished school and I'm looking for a summer _____ in Canada.

2. I am very interested in learning something about the _____ and life in Canada.

3. I need to find an agency that helps me to _____ information and the necessary documents.

4. Fortunately my parents will _____ my trip and my stay.

5. I'd like to _____ in a hotel or a restaurant.

6. During my stay I would also like to _____ much of Canada's wildlife.

4.2 Work and Travel in Canada – Part 2

Complete the following text (sentences 1–6) with <u>suitable</u> words.

1. You don't need any qualifications or _____ because training will be given.

2. There are a lot of different possibilities: you may _____ as a sales-assistant, cashier, waiter in a restaurant or in an entertainment park.

3. You get a visa that allows you to _____ in Canada for an extra month.
4. Also, it is only a short journey if you want to _____ the USA.
5. The agencies will _____ the necessary documents for your stay.
6. They will help you to solve any _____ you might have during your stay in Canada.

Aufgabe 5: Schreiben

You are planning to work abroad for a year after leaving school. On the Internet you have found the following job advertisements.

- *Read the job advertisements.*
- *Choose one job you want to apply for.*

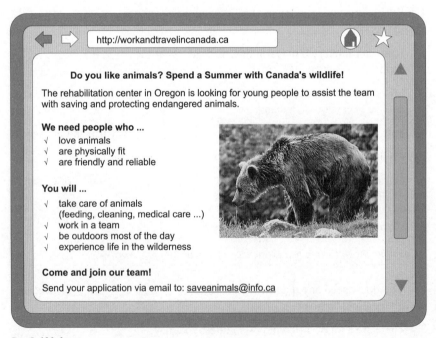

Bär © 123rf.com

or

Global Volunteering Placements in Vancouver

Get to know one of the most beautiful cities in the world and work as an assistant in a day-care-center for children from 3–6 years.

We are looking for young volunteers who ...
- √ are friendly and reliable
- √ are responsible and self-organized
- √ love to work and play with kids

You will ...
- √ get to know a new culture by playing with children
- √ read books, tell stories and do a lot of outdoor activities
- √ meet young people from all over the world

Please send your application to Vancouver-childcare@info.ca

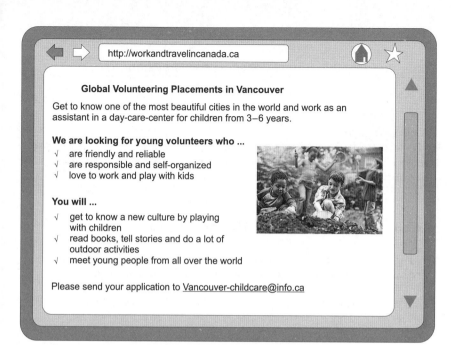

spielende Kinder © Cade Martin, Dawn Arlotta

Write your <u>email application</u> for <u>the job you choose</u>.
Include the following information:
- *your personal details*
- *your general interests*
- *your motivation especially for this job*
- *your qualifications*

Write about <u>120 words and use your own words</u>. Remember the formals aspects.

Lösungsvorschläge

Erster Prüfungsteil: Hörverstehen – Leseverstehen

> *Hauptschulabschluss Haupttermin*
>
> *Wichtige Hinweise:*
> *Alle Texte, die im Folgenden zu hören sind, werden zweimal vorgespielt. Vor dem ersten Hören wird Zeit gegeben, sich mit den Aufgaben vertraut zu machen.*
> *Der Hörverstehenstest besteht aus zwei Teilen:*

Aufgabe 1: Hörverstehen Teil 1: *The Thames Tunnel*

> *You are going to hear an interview with Melinda Gordon and Thomas Carrey. They talk about something that once was called the 8th Wonder of the World: the Thames Tunnel.*
> *First read the tasks. Then listen to the interview. While you are listening, tick the correct box or write down the information needed. At the end you will hear the interview again. Now read the tasks. You have 1 minute to do this.*
>
> *Now listen to the interview and do the tasks.*

1 MELINDA GORDON: Hello, you are listening to BBC radio one. I'm Melinda Gordon. Did you know that it was 200 years ago that people started to build a tunnel under the river Thames? Thomas Carrey, an expert on historic monuments can tell us more about this enormous project.

5 THOMAS CARREY: Yes. The harbour of London was the busiest in the world. Every day thousands of ships came in. All the things they brought to London had to be transported from north to south. At that time there was only one bridge across the river: London Bridge. But it was too far away from the harbour. And constructing a new bridge would have brought the ship traffic
10 to a standstill.
That's why they needed another way to cross the river, you see ... So the idea of a tunnel was born. But in those days, people thought it was impossible to build a tunnel under water. It was a Frenchman, Marc Brunel, who finally wanted to try it.

15 MELINDA GORDON: Wow, that was quite courageous – without today's technology!
THOMAS CARREY: The biggest problem was the earth falling down on the people who worked underground. Brunel invented a machine to support the walls and the roof while the men dug the tunnel. It allowed 36 men to work at the

same time. They started in 1825, but still it was dangerous. The air underground was a problem, it was bad and so the workers often had to be brought up into the fresh air.

MELINDA GORDON: Oh, that doesn't sound like an easy job ...

THOMAS CARREY: No, not at all! It was also wet, because water came in from the river. At that time all kinds of dirt were thrown into the river. Just imagine how awful this water was!

MELINDA GORDON: Oh, what horrible conditions!

THOMAS CARREY: And there were even explosions and the water from the river flooded into the tunnel so that the workers had to run for their lives.

MELINDA GORDON: Ach, oh. But at last in 1843 the tunnel opened ...

THOMAS CARREY: Exactly. But at that time it was only possible to *walk* through it because there were no proper roads for the horse-drawn carriages. Building the tunnel had been so expensive that there was simply no money left to build the two large roads that the horses needed to transport goods through the tunnel. People, however, could simply use the stairs to get down.

So during the first years the tunnel was just a tourist attraction. Thousands of people came to visit it. For people at that time the first tunnel under a river was like the 8th Wonder of the World. In 1852 there was even the world's first underwater fair inside the Thames Tunnel. Can you imagine fire-eaters, artists, Indian dancers and Chinese singers presenting a show in the tunnel?

MELINDA GORDON: But of course the original idea of the tunnel was to transport things from one side of the Thames to the other and not to be a tourist attraction. What happened?

THOMAS CARREY: Well – you see it took some more years before in 1865 the tunnel was ready for what it had been made for: carrying things across the river – but now by *train*!

MELINDA GORDON: And today the Thames Tunnel is still part of the London Transport. It belongs to the London railway network. Go to London, just get on the Circle Line train and you will enjoy a ride through the 8th World Wonder of the 19th century!

> Now listen to the interview again and check your answers.

1. c
   Hinweis: At that time there was only one bridge across the river: London Bridge." (Z. 7f.)

2. a) no modern technology/earth falling down on the people who worked underground/
   Hinweis: "... without today's technology! ... The biggest problem was the earth falling down on the people who worked underground." (Z. 15ff.)
   b) bad air/explosions/tunnel flooded with water from the river/workers had to run for their lives
   Hinweis: "The air underground was a problem ... And there were even explosions and the water from the river flooded into the tunnel so that the workers had to run for their lives." (Z. 20ff.)

3. b
   Hinweis: "... only possible to <u>walk</u> through it because there were no proper roads for the horse-drawn carriages." (Z. 31f.)

4. fire-eaters/artists/Indian dancers/Chinese singers/shows
   Hinweis: "Can you imagine fire-eaters, artists, Indian dancers and Chinese singers presenting a show in the tunnel?" (Z. 39f.)

5. carrying things across the river (by train)
   Hinweis: "... in 1865 the tunnel was ready for what it had been made for: carrying things across the river – but now by train!" (Z. 44ff.)

Aufgabe 2: Hörverstehen Teil 2: *How to join Canada's RCMP*

> *Police officer Bill Fordy informs students at Surrey High School about how to start a career with the Royal Canadian Mounted Police, who are called Mounties. Student leader Alex Smith asks him some questions.*
> *First read the tasks. Then listen to the interview. While you are listening, tick the correct box or write down the information needed. At the end you will hear the interview again. Now read the tasks. You have <u>1 minute</u> to do this.*
> *Now listen to the interview and do the tasks.*

ALEX SMITH: Welcome, Mr Fordy.
BILL FORDY: Hello.
ALEX SMITH: Nice to have you with us today.
BILL FORDY: Thank you.

ALEX SMITH: Can you as a police officer tell us what it takes for someone to join the Royal Canadian Mounted Police and to become a Mountie?

BILL FORDY: Hmmm, well that's a question I've been asked a lot of times. Basically, the RCMP is looking for highly motivated team players with leadership qualities who care about law and order in society. We need strong, honest and respectable characters, who can make decisions and take over responsibility in difficult and often dangerous situations.

ALEX SMITH: Yeah, well, sure! And, can just anybody join the RCMP?

BILL FORDY: No, not anybody of course. To start with, as an RCMP officer you must be a Canadian citizen. If you were born outside Canada, you must have full Canadian citizenship before applying to the RCMP. And of course it's important that you can speak and write both official languages – English and French – fluently.

ALEX SMITH: Right. That sounds sensible – but what about other qualifications that are needed?

BILL FORDY: Well, you can apply to the RCMP and do some basic training at the age of 18. But you can't work for us before you are 19 years old. And you do need a secondary school qualification and should have a driver's license.

ALEX SMITH: Oh, I see. So much for the conditions to get into the job. But what's interesting for our young listeners – what is the job like in reality? I mean, what about the everyday routine?

BILL FORDY: Ah, well, hm. Police work always sounds exciting and all that, but in reality it is exhausting, too. Police work is hard physical work. It is extremely important to have a high level of fitness before you apply to the RCMP. You know, our training program is not designed to get you into shape, but rather to prepare you for the tough job. You must be able to run after thieves, to handle aggressive people. And you'll have to assist injured and bleeding people in need. And this isn't even the most stressful part of our job. Look, as a police officer you need to carry a firearm and you might have to use it to save your own life or someone else's. This is something all Mounties are worried about very much.

ALEX SMITH: Oh yes, I see. I can understand those worries very well. What else do you think young people should know when they want to apply?

BILL FORDY: Well, to become a Mountie you must be willing to spend six months at the RCMP Academy in Regina. You'll have to study hard and attend classes that train you for policing. And you cannot choose where – that means in which region or town – you want to work. You will be sent to a police department in Canada where your helping hand is needed the most! This is one of the biggest challenges for RCMP applicants. Another challenge is the shift work. Policing takes place 24 hours a day. So, you must be ready to work at changing times night and day.

ALEX SMITH: All right now, I can see the hard part of the job – but still, I'd like to join the RCMP – what are the next steps?
BILL FORDY: If you want to apply and get first-hand information from one of our police officers go to a career presentation in your town or city. And on our website you'll find more details about the application process.
ALEX SMITH: Wow, that was very interesting. Thanks a lot. It was a pleasure to have you with us.

Now listen to the interview again and check your answers.

---

1. highly motivated / team players / leadership qualities / care about law and order / high level of fitness / strong / honest / respectable characters / make decisions / take over responsibility
   Hinweis: "... the RCMP is looking for highly motivated team players with leadership qualities who care about law and order in society. We need strong, honest and respectable characters, who can make decisions and take over responsibility in difficult and often dangerous situations." (Z. 8 ff.)

2. b
   Hinweis: "... as an RCMP officer you must be a Canadian citizen." (Z. 13 f.)

3. c
   Hinweis: "... you do need a secondary school qualification ..." (Z. 21 f.)

4. c
   Hinweis: "... to prepare you for the tough job." (Z. 30)

5. a
   Hinweis: "... as a police officer you need to carry a firearm and you might have to use it to save your own life or someone else's. This is something all Mounties are worried about very much." (Z. 33 ff.)

6. c
   Hinweis: "You'll have to study hard and attend classes that train you for policing." (Z. 39 f.)

Ende des Hörverstehenstests.

Aufgabe 3: Leseverstehen

1. ... daughter
   Hinweis: "Being the daughter of Dr. Emma Hart wasn't always easy." (Z. 3f.)

2. false
   because the text says "Mom was running a 'call-in show' on a radio/she talked to people on the phone who asked her to help them with their problems." (Z. 4 ff.)

3. false
   because the text says "She was calling them her 'wounded birds' – not during the show, of course, and never to anyone but me." (Z. 9 ff.)

4. false
   because the text says "I had no major crisis ..." (Z. 19)

5. ... that her mother had no time for her/her mother was always busy.
   Hinweis: "To me it sometimes felt like she spent much more time caring for her patients than caring for me, her daughter." (Z. 13 ff.)

6. true
   because the text says "If anybody can call her, well, why can't I, her own daughter?" (Z. 35 f.)

7. false
   because the text says "'When Mom got home that evening I knew it wasn't going to work" (Z. 63 f.) / "She was very busy with her own problems and wouldn't listen to me', I said." (Z. 72 f.)

8. Amanda used the expression "wounded birds".
   Hinweis: "'You know, the thing about my mother is that she has all these wounded birds who take all the time she has.'" (Z. 76 ff.)

Zweiter Prüfungsteil: Wortschatz – Schreiben

Aufgabe 4: Wortschatz

4.1 Work and Travel in Canada – Part 1

1. I've just finished school and I'm looking for a summer **job** in Canada.

2. I am very interested in learning something about the **culture** and life in Canada.

3. I need to find an agency that helps me to **get** information and the necessary documents.
4. Fortunately my parents will **sponsor** my trip and my stay.
5. I'd like to **work** in a hotel or a restaurant.
6. During my stay I would also like to **see** much of Canada's wildlife.

4.2 Part 2

1. You don't need any qualifications or **experience** because training will be given.
2. There are a lot of different possibilities: you may **work** as a sales-assistant, cashier, waiter in a restaurant or in an entertainment park.
3. You get a visa that allows you to **travel/stay** in Canada for an extra month.
4. Also, it is only a short journey if you want to **visit/go to** the USA.
5. The agencies will **organise/take care of** the necessary documents for your stay.
6. They will help you to solve any **problems** you might have during your stay in Canada.

Aufgabe 5: Schreiben

Hinweis: Hier ist es wichtig, dass du dir die Aufgabenstellung und beide Anzeigen genau durchliest, bevor du anfängst zu schreiben. Entscheide dich für <u>eine</u> Anzeige. Achte darauf, dass auch eine Bewerbung per E-Mail den formalen Aspekten eines Bewerbungsschreibens entsprechen muss.

1. Schreibe zu allen genannten Punkten etwas: Angaben zur Person, allgemeine Interessen, dein Interesse für genau diesen Job, deine Qualifikationen
2. Finde einen passenden Anfang (Begrüßungsformel) und ein passendes Ende (Schlussformel).
3. Schreibe auf jeden Fall mehr als 120 Wörter.
4. Schreibe deine E-Mail in ganzen Sätzen. Achte dabei auf die formalen Aspekte. Verwende dabei auch die Langformen, z. B. "I am" statt "I'm".

Nutze beim Schreiben, falls nötig, die Formulierungen der Wortschatzaufgaben 4.1 und 4.2. Sie können beim Verfassen deines Textes hilfreich sein.

Beispiellösung Anzeige 1:

Dear Sir or Madam,

My name is Metin Ucar and I am 15 years old. I live in Krefeld, Germany. I am very interested in the job at your rehabilitation center in Oregon because I love animals. At home I often take care of our two dogs and our rabbit. One of my favourite subjects at school is Biology. Protecting wildlife and endangered animals is very important to me. Therefore, I would like to apply for the job at your center. As I have never been to your country before, I would love to go there. I can start on July 1st.
In my free time I also help my parents in our garden, so I am used to working outside. Last autumn I did an internship at a garden center. I loved working in a team, and I was told that I was a friendly and reliable employee.
Working in your center, I could help you with your work and learn a lot about saving wildlife.

I am looking forward to hearing from you.

Yours faithfully,
Metin Ucar   *(179 words)*

Beispiellösung Anzeige 2:

Dear Sir or Madam,

In response to your advertisement, I would like to apply for the job as an assistant at your day-care-center. My name is Celine Müller, I am 16 years old and I live in Hilden, Germany.
My hobbies are martial arts and meeting friends. I am in a judo team and I take part in tournaments. I have to be very organised in order to coordinate my schoolwork with the tournaments.
I am very motivated to do the job at your day-care-center because my qualifications match your requirements perfectly. In spring I worked in a kindergarten for three weeks. I loved playing with the children, and it was a very important experience for me to take responsibility. I now know that I want to work with children in the future.
Apart from speaking English, I am a native speaker of German and have some knowledge of Polish because my mother is from Poland. I would love working together with people from all over the world.

I am looking forward to hearing from you.

Yours faithfully,
Celine Müller   *(180 words)*

Zentrale Prüfung am Ende der Klasse 10 – NRW – Hauptschulabschluss – Englisch 2017

Erster Prüfungsteil: Hörverstehen – Leseverstehen

Aufgabe 1: Hörverstehen Teil 1

Hamba Kahle Nelson Mandela

You are going to hear a speech by Kumi Naidoo (a human rights activist from South Africa) on the death of Nelson Mandela.

- First read the tasks.
- Then listen to the speech.
- While you are listening, tick the correct box **or** write down the information needed.
- At the end you will hear the speech again.
- Now read the tasks. You have <u>1 minute</u> to do this.

Now listen to the speech and do the tasks.

1. According to the speaker, Nelson Mandela ...
   a) ☐ fought in a war.
   b) ☐ sometimes faked his identity.
   c) ☐ was tolerated by the police at first.

2. In his teenage years, the speaker ...
   a) ☐ worked at Mandela's side.
   b) ☐ went to a school for white kids.
   c) ☐ protested about unfair school conditions.

3. At a hotel, Mandela went to the kitchen. Say **why**.

   _____

4. When the speaker took children to Mandela, they ...
   a) ☐ were afraid of the speaker.
   b) ☐ wanted a picture with Mandela.
   c) ☐ thought Mandela would not have time.

5. When Mandela joined the children, he thanked them. Say **for what**.

   _____

The following task is about **the whole speech**:

6. The speech is about …
   a) ☐ what Mandela did against racism.
   b) ☐ how Mandela spent his time in jail.
   c) ☐ the fact that Mandela was a great man.

Aufgabe 2: Hörverstehen Teil 2

Welcome to Europe?

You are going to hear a radio interview. Sally Wilson from BBC Radio 4 interviews Clara Travers, a human rights activist, about her current job.

> - First read the tasks.
> - Then listen to the interview.
> - While you are listening, tick the correct box or write down the information needed.
> - At the end you will hear the interview again.
> - Now read the tasks. You have <u>1 minute</u> to do this.

Now listen to the interview and do the tasks.

1. Clara's main task at sea is to …
   a) ☐ help people in danger.
   b) ☐ coordinate her crew's work.
   c) ☐ show boats the way to a harbour.

2. One morning, there was a boat with problems. Name **one** problem.
   _____

3. The people on the boat …
   a) ☐ were male adults.
   b) ☐ got to a safe place later on.
   c) ☐ ate something on the rescue boat.

4. In Turkey, the people had had to …
   a) ☐ wait for two months.
   b) ☐ pay for their sea passage.
   c) ☐ leave their belongings behind.

5. Clara mentions four ideals which are important in Europe. Write down **one**.
   _____

The following task is about **the whole interview**:

6. Clara gives this interview to …
   a) ☐ raise money for her work.
   b) ☐ complain about her hard job.
   c) ☐ tell people that refugees need help.

Aufgabe 3: Leseverstehen

A New Home by Dorothy Dyer

Babalwa lay in bed next to her cousin. Outside her aunt's house there were unfamiliar sounds: taxis hooting[1], people shouting and music pumping from the club at the end of the road. They weren't the sounds of the rural village she had come from. No, she was in the big city, like she had wanted to be. And she hated it.

The first day at her cousin's school had been a nightmare[2]. Her cousin hadn't introduced her to anybody. In fact, she had turned her back on Babalwa to speak with her friends. They had whispered and giggled and Babalwa had been sure they were talking about her.

Why had she ever asked to come to the city? Why had she begged her mother to send her?

"Wake up, Babalwa!" She felt someone poking[3] her shoulder. "Wake up, you lazy girl! Your mother promised us you would work hard in the house. Get up and make porridge for breakfast." Babalwa's aunt was shouting in her ear.

Babalwa sat up, bumping[4] her cousin who groaned[5] and rolled over. "Be careful, you clumsy[6] girl. Don't wake up Sisipho. She needs her beauty sleep," hissed her aunt.

In the kitchen Babalwa stirred the porridge on the stove. Her eyes were burning with tiredness.

"I'm hungry," Sisipho said, coming up behind Babalwa.

"Babalwa will serve you, my baby, sit down," her mother said. Babalwa turned to look at the two of them, waiting to be served.

"I am not your servant," she said, "I will not serve my own cousin."

This was when her aunt started shouting at her.

"You do not talk to me like that. Do you hear me?" She looked furious. "I knew this was a bad idea, letting you come and stay in our house. Is your mother paying me for your keep? No. I'm going to tell her what an ungrateful girl you are."

Babalwa couldn't believe her aunt was like this. Whenever she had visited before she had been friendly and kind. Still, she wasn't ready to be sent back to her village. "I am sorry, Auntie," she said softly, thinking of her mother.

Babalwa spooned out porridge into the bowls and she felt bitterness in her heart.

At her village Babalwa had shared a room with her mother and two cousins. Until she came to her aunt's house she couldn't imagine living in a place with a bathroom inside the house with taps for hot and cold water. At her village if they wanted water they had to fetch it. It was a long walk to the river and it was freezing in the winter.

Babalwa thought of her friend, Anathi, at her village. They had been friends from when they were little and knew each other inside out. Where was Anathi at this moment? She had been angry when Babalwa had decided to go to Cape Town – they had even fought about it. But then they had cried and laughed together, and promised to stay friends forever. Anathi had told her Cape Town was horrible and Babalwa hadn't believed her. But maybe she was right.

---

1 to hoot – to sound a car horn
2 nightmare – a bad dream
3 to poke – to push your finger into someone/something
4 to bump – *etwas oder jemanden (hier: mit dem Körper) anstoßen*
5 to groan – *stöhnen, ächzen, seufzen*
6 clumsy – *ungeschickt, tollpatschig*

adapted from: "Two-faced friends" chapter 1 by Dorothy Dyer, https://live.fundza.mobi/home/library/fiction-books/two-faced-friends/chapter-1/

> *Tick the correct box <u>and</u> support your answer by quoting from the text where required.*

1. Babalwa is used to the noises she hears outside.

   This statement is

   a) ☐ true   b) ☐ false

   Evidence from the text: _____

2. On her first day at her cousin's school Babalwa …
   a) ☐ felt welcome and accepted.
   b) ☐ was completely on her own.
   c) ☐ could only talk with her cousin.

3. Her aunt expects Babalwa to help with the housework.

   This statement is

   a) ☐ true   b) ☐ false

   Evidence from the text: _____

4. Babalwa's cousin Sisipho is treated like a … by Babalwa's aunt.
   a) ☐ slave
   b) ☐ princess
   c) ☐ newborn

   Evidence from the text: _____

5. Her aunt treated Babalwa differently in the past.

   This statement is

   a) ☐ true   b) ☐ false

   Evidence from the text: _____

6. At her aunt's house, Babalwa's standard of living is …
   a) ☐ better than before.
   b) ☐ worse than before.
   c) ☐ the same as before.

   Evidence from the text: _____

7. When Anathi heard of Babalwa's plans, she …
   a) ☐ was happy for her.
   b) ☐ ended their friendship.
   c) ☐ warned her about the city.

   Evidence from the text: _____

Zweiter Prüfungsteil: Wortschatz – Schreiben

Aufgabe 4: Wortschatz

4.1 Teenage Life in South Africa – Part 1

The following text is about school in South Africa.

- Complete the following text (sentences 1–6) with words from the box.
- Use each word only <u>once</u>.
- There is <u>one more word</u> than you need.

begin	education	grade	little	receive	public	wear

1. In South Africa, school years _____ in January and have four blocks.

2. South African children must go to school until they are 15. Many of them go to large _____ schools.

3. For people from the age of 16, further _____ is usually optional.

4. Most schools _____ money from the state to pay for their costs, but they also charge school fees.

5. However, poor families usually only pay _____ money for school – less than rich families, at least.

6. But on top of that, pupils must _____ school uniforms, which can be very expensive.

4.2 Teenage Life in South Africa – Part 2

The following sentences are school rules for pupils at a South African high school.

Complete the following text (sentences 1–6) with <u>suitable</u> words.

1. All teachers and other pupils must be treated with _____ at all times.

2. All pupils must _____ the school building no later than 8:00.

3. Latecomers' names are recorded. They need to stay for an _____ hour after school.

4. Pupils must give their full _____ to every lesson. Talking, making noise etc. is forbidden during the lesson.

5. Play-fighting is strictly forbidden because it can _____ real fighting.

6. All _____ of make-up are not allowed. Hair must be neat and clean. Clothing other than school uniform is forbidden.

Aufgabe 5: Schreiben

Your school has a partner school in South Africa. A group of pupils from your partner school is going to visit your own school in a few weeks.
Everyone in your class has been given a "partner" from this group of pupils. Yours is Lisha, a teenage girl. You want to know a little bit about her before her visit.

> Write an <u>email</u> to Lisha. In the email, please …
>
> (1) … write about:
> - your school
> - a typical school day
> - (what is special about) the city/town/village you live in
>
> and say what you **like** or **don't like** about these things.
>
> (2) … ask what you would like to know about:
> - Lisha herself
> - school life in South Africa
>
> Remember to write a nice beginning and a friendly ending.
> Write about 120 words.

Lösungsvorschläge

Erster Prüfungsteil: Hörverstehen – Leseverstehen

Hauptschulabschluss Haupttermin
Wichtige Hinweise:
Alle Texte, die im Folgenden zu hören sind, werden zweimal vorgespielt. Vor dem ersten Hören wird Zeit gegeben, sich mit den Aufgaben vertraut zu machen.
Der Hörverstehenstest besteht aus zwei Teilen:

Aufgabe 1: Hörverstehen Teil 1: *Hamba Kahle Nelson Mandela*

You are going to hear a speech by Kumi Naidoo (a human rights activist from South Africa) on the death of Nelson Mandela.
First read the tasks. Then listen to the speech. While you are listening, tick the correct box or write down the information needed. At the end you will hear the speech again. Now read the tasks. You have 1 minute to do this.
Now listen to the speech and do the tasks.

1 The world has lost a true leader, a true father and a true role model. Nelson Mandela is dead.
    He was a fighter against racism in South Africa. He often had to hide from the police, make people think he was someone else. Mandela also had to stay in prison
5 for 27 years! But in 1994, Nelson Mandela became the first black president of South Africa. His example helped me and thousands of others become stronger in our fight against racism.
    As a teenager, I fought against racism in schools – in fact, the schooling for black kids was far worse than the schooling for white kids. At that time I learned
10 a lot about what Mandela had done in his fight against racism. From then on, Mandela became an important role model for me. Fighting against bad things in the world has become my life, too.
    Later in life, I had the chance to meet Nelson Mandela a few times. I first met him at a hotel in 1993. After lunch on that day, he asked the manager of the hotel
15 if he could thank the people who had made the food. He went to the kitchen and greeted everyone. I saw him shake everyone's hands, one by one – a simple, honest action that meant so much to all of the workers.
    In 1995, I met him again. I took some kids to Parliament to meet Mandela. They were excited to have a photo taken with him. They kept asking me what they

20 should say and how they should prepare for talking to him. Gosh, were they nervous! But then Nelson Mandela walked in … and the first thing he did was: thank everyone! Yes, the President of South Africa thanked everyone for being there. "I know how busy you all are and I thank you for taking time to meet me," he said. At that moment everyone understood what he wanted to tell them: He was just a
25 human being, a person like them, and everyone relaxed.

Nelson Mandela once said that the fight for justice is not easy. He is a symbol of hope in a world full of bad things. All over Africa, Nelson Mandela was a hero! Today he is also a hero in the rest of the world. His ideas will live on in my heart.

Hamba Kahle – Rest in peace Nelson Mandela, you have more than earned it!

> *Now listen to the speech again and check your answers.*

1. b
   Hinweis: "He often had to hide from the police, make people think he was someone else." (Z. 3 f.)

2. c
   Hinweis: "As a teenager, I fought against racism in schools – …" (Z. 8)

3. to thank the people who had made the food / to thank the kitchen staff / to thank for the food / to greet everyone (in the kitchen)
   Hinweis: "… if he could thank the people who had made the food. He went to the kitchen and greeted everyone. I saw him shake everyone's hands, …" (Z. 15 f.)

4. b
   Hinweis: "They were excited to have a photo taken with him." (Z. 19)

5. (for) being there / meeting him / taking (their) time (to meet him) / coming
   Hinweis: "… thanked everyone for being there. '… I thank you for taking time to meet me' …" (Z. 22 f.)

6. c
   Hinweis: "All over Africa, Nelson Mandela was <u>a hero</u>! Today he is also a hero in the rest of the world." (Z. 27 f.)

Aufgabe 2: Hörverstehen Teil 2: *Welcome to Europe?*

You are going to hear a radio interview. Sally Wilson from BBC Radio 4 interviews Clara Travers, a human rights activist, about her current job.
First read the tasks. Then listen to the interview. While you are listening, tick the correct box or write down the information needed. At the end you will hear the interview again. Now read the tasks. You have 1 minute to do this.
Now listen to the interview and do the tasks.

SALLY: Hello and welcome back. You are listening to BBC Radio 4. I'm Sally Wilson. With me today is Clara Travers, a human rights activist from the UK. She currently works off the Greek coast as part of a team that helps refugees. Hello Clara, it's awfully nice to have you here. What can you tell us about your job?

CLARA: Hello Sally, thanks for having me. The most important part of my work is to ensure the safety of life at sea, which means rescuing anyone in trouble. We also try to guide boats away from dangerous landing sites. That's part of our watch operation.

SALLY: Can you give us an example of what your job is like at the moment?

CLARA: Yes, I remember one morning in December last year very well. We were on standby and then ... we got the call! A boat had been spotted.

SALLY: And, er, did you manage to reach the boat in time?

CLARA: Yep, as soon as we got to the small boat we realized how bad the conditions were: it was a very small boat, actually a rubber dinghy of very poor quality – and it was overfilled with 52 Syrians. We could see immediately it was going to sink. We had to act very quickly and started helping people onto our boat.

SALLY: So ... were you able to get everyone onboard safe and sound?

CLARA: Yes! There were babies, children, women and men, but everyone was able to get onboard safely. Some felt cold or had got wet. We explained to them that we would take them safely to Greece where they would get dry clothes and something to eat and drink.

SALLY: How did this group manage to get on that small boat in the first place?

CLARA: It took this group of refugees two months of walking before they got to the Turkish coast. In Turkey they paid a lot of money to people smugglers because they needed the chance to get a boat to cross the sea between Turkey and Greece. They carried only small bags with a few personal belongings and ... they made it!

SALLY: Why is it so important to help refugees in trouble?

CLARA: It's the sheer numbers! Every day there are hundreds, sometimes thousands of refugees landing on the beaches around the Greek islands. Remember what Europe stands for: respect, freedom, democracy and universal human rights. I believe in these things. That's why I help in Greece, hoping for a better future.

SALLY: Well, thanks for this very interesting interview, Clara, and all the best to you!

CLARA: Thank you, goodbye.

> Now listen to the interview again and check your answers.

1. a
   Hinweis: "The most important part of my work is to ensure the safety of life at sea, ..." (Z. 6f.)

2. boat too small/of poor quality/overfilled/going to sink
   Hinweis: "... it was a very small boat, actually a rubber dinghy of very poor quality – and it was overfilled with 52 Syrians. We could see immediately it was going to sink." (Z. 15ff.)

3. b
   Hinweis: "... we would take them safely to Greece where they would get dry clothes and something to eat and drink." (Z. 22f.)

4. b
   Hinweis: "In Turkey they paid a lot of money to people smugglers ... to get a boat to cross the sea ..." (Z. 26f.)

5. respect/freedom/democracy/human rights
   Hinweis: "Remember what Europe stands for: respect, freedom, democracy and universal human rights." (Z. 32ff.)

6. c
   Hinweis: "Every day there are hundreds, sometimes thousands of refugees landing on the beaches around the Greek islands. ... That's why I help in Greece, ..." (Z. 31ff.)

> Ende des Hörverstehenstests.

Aufgabe 3: Leseverstehen

1. false
   Evidence from the text: Outside her aunt's house there were unfamiliar sounds. (Z. 3 f.) / They weren't the sounds of the rural village she had come from. (Z. 6 ff.)

2. b
   Hinweis: "Her cousin hadn't introduced her to anybody. In fact, she had turned her back on Babalwa to speak with her friends." (Z. 12 ff.)

3. true
   Evidence from the text: "Your mother promised us you would work hard in the house. Get up and make porridge for breakfast." (Z. 23 ff.)

4. b
   Evidence from the text: "Don't wake up Sisipho. She needs her beauty sleep," hissed her aunt. (Z. 29 ff.) / "Babalwa will serve you, (my baby, sit down.)" (Z. 37 f.)

5. true
   Evidence from the text: Whenever she had visited before she had been friendly and kind. (Z. 53 f.)

6. a
   Evidence from the text: At her village Babalwa had shared a room with her mother and two cousins. / Until she came to her aunt's house she couldn't imagine living in a place with a bathroom inside the house with taps for hot and cold water. / At her village if they wanted water they had to fetch it. (It was a long walk to the river and it was freezing in the winter.) (Z. 61 ff.)

7. c
   Evidence from the text: Anathi had told her Cape Town was horrible … (Z. 79 f.)

Zweiter Prüfungsteil: Wortschatz – Schreiben

Aufgabe 4: Wortschatz

4.1 Teenage Life in South Africa – Part 1

1. In South Africa, school years **begin** in January and have four blocks.

2. South African children must go to school until they are 15. Many of them go to large **public** schools.

3. For people from the age of 16, further **education** is usually optional.

4. Most schools **receive** money from the state to pay for their costs, but they also charge school fees.

5. However, poor families usually only pay **little** money for school – less than rich families, at least.

6. But on top of that, pupils must **wear** school uniforms, which can be very expensive.

4.2 Teenage Life in South Africa – Part 2

1. All teachers and other pupils must be treated with **respect / politeness** at all times.

2. All pupils must **be in / arrive at / enter / reach** the school building no later than 8:00.

3. Latecomers' names are recorded. They need to stay for an **extra / additional** hour after school.

4. Pupils must give their full **attention / concentration** to every lesson. Talking, making noise etc. is forbidden during the lesson.

5. Play-fighting is strictly forbidden because it can **become / end in / lead to / cause** real fighting.

6. All **kinds / forms** of make-up are not allowed. Hair must be neat and clean. Clothing other than school uniform is forbidden.

Aufgabe 5: Schreiben

Hinweis: Lies die Aufgabenstellung genau durch, bevor du anfängst zu schreiben. Achte darauf, dass es sich um eine E-Mail an eine Austauschschülerin, Lisha, aus Südafrika handelt und du somit eine persönliche Mail schreibst.

1. *Schreibe etwas zu <u>allen Aspekten</u>:*
   - *Über deine Schule, einen typischen Schultag, und was du an deiner Heimatstadt magst oder nicht magst.*
   - *Stelle Lisha Fragen über sie selbst und über das Schulleben in Südafrika.*
2. *Beginne die Mail mit einer netten, persönlichen Begrüßung und runde deinen Text mit einem freundlichen Schluss ab.*
3. *Schreibe um die 120 Wörter – es können aber auch mehr sein.*
4. *Schreibe deine E-Mail in ganzen Sätzen.*

Beispiellösung:

Dear Lisha,

My name is Clara Schneider and I'm 16 years old. I'm really looking forward to your visit at our school in a few weeks. I've never met anyone from South Africa before, and I know only little about your country.

There are 350 students at our school, which is in Monheim, a small town between Cologne and Düsseldorf. I usually get up at 7 o'clock and leave for school at about 7:45. I can walk there and don't have to take the bus. School begins at 8:15. We have a breakfast break at 9:45 and a one-hour lunch break at 12:45. In the afternoon, we have school till 3:30 pm.

Monheim is a small town, so a lot of people know each other. I like that. We also have cafés, a swimming pool and some other places to go in our free time, but we don't have a cinema or big shops. That's what I don't like because I have to take a train to Cologne to go shopping or watch the latest films.

What about you, Lisha? What are your hobbies? What do you like or don't like? Do you live in a big or small town? How is school life in South Africa? Do you have any favourite subjects? Which language do you speak at school? At our school we learned some facts about the history of your country. Do you still feel the effect of apartheid at your school, for example?

I look forward to hearing from you.

Take care!
Clara   *(256 words)*

Notizen

Notizen

Ihre Meinung zählt!

Liebe Kundin, lieber Kunde,

der STARK Verlag hat das Ziel, Sie effektiv beim Lernen zu unterstützen. In welchem Maße uns dies gelingt, wissen Sie am besten. Deshalb bitten wir Sie, uns Ihre Meinung zu den STARK-Produkten in dieser Umfrage mitzuteilen.

www.stark-verlag.de/ihremeinung

Illustration: mecaleha, ArtLana (Thinkstock)

www.stark-verlag.de

STARK

Der Weg zur besseren Note

Dieser Button zeigt bei jeder Produktreihe an, auf welcher Lernphase der Schwerpunkt liegt.

Abschlussprüfung

Anhand von Original-Aufgaben die Prüfungssituation trainieren. Schülergerechte Lösungen helfen bei der Leistungskontrolle.

Training

Prüfungsrelevantes Wissen schülergerecht präsentiert. Übungsaufgaben mit Lösungen sichern den Lernerfolg.

Klassenarbeiten

Praxisnahe Übungen für eine gezielte Vorbereitung auf Klassenarbeiten.

STARK in Klassenarbeiten

Schülergerechtes Training wichtiger Themenbereiche für mehr Lernerfolg und bessere Noten.

Kompakt-Wissen

Kompakte Darstellung des prüfungsrelevanten Wissens zum schnellen Nachschlagen und Wiederholen.

Und vieles mehr auf www.stark-verlag.de

STARK

Abschluss in der Tasche – und dann?

In den **STARK** Ratgebern findest du alle Informationen für einen erfolgreichen Start in die berufliche Zukunft.

www.stark-verlag.de

STARK